REPENT
AND
BELIEVE

REPENT
AND
BELIEVE

The Celebration of the
Sacrament of Penance

Edited by

Rev. William Freburger

AVE MARIA PRESS
Notre Dame, Indiana 46556

Nihil Obstat: John L. Reedy, C.S.C.
            Censor Deputatus

Imprimatur: Most Rev. Leo A. Pursley, D.D.
             Bishop of Fort Wayne/South Bend

First edition, September 1971

Second edition, 1972. Published by
Ave Maria Press, Notre Dame, Indiana

Photography: 8, Marne Breckensiek
             18, 79, Anthony Rowland
             37, 90, Richard Clapper
             53, Vern Sigl

Printed in the United States of America

Contents

Introduction 6

1. Penance: Scripture and Tradition 9

2. Penance: The Present Situation 14

3. Guidelines for Parish Celebrations of Penance 19

4. Preparation of Children for Penance 32

5. Celebrations of Penance for Various Age Levels 38

   Primary Grades
   Sixth Grade
   Eighth Grade—Christmas
   Junior High
   General Penance Service—I
   General Penance Service—II

6. Lenten Penitential Programs 54

   First Session—Fourth Week of Lent
   Second Session—Fifth Week of Lent
   Third Session—Wednesday of Holy Week
   A General Holy Week Service
   Good Friday

7. A Penitential-Eucharistic Service 75

8. Special Theme Penance Services 80

   Return to the Lord
   God's Peace
   The Spirit of Forgiveness
   Dedication to Service
   Reconciliation
   God's Mercy and Love

Appendix: A Pastoral Letter on Public Penance 91

Introduction

A nationally prominent liturgist recently described the sacrament of Penance as "a casualty of renewal." Indeed, it is no secret that confession habits among Catholics have changed—for the worse, some think. Any of us can document the externals of the change from our own personal experience: outside the confessional, the lines are shorter; inside, "the time since my last confession" is longer! The process has taken shape and assumed conscious proportions during the last decade; but the customary listing of causes—change in the Church, laxity of religious education, the "new morality," a lack of piety and conviction, etc.—always omits a factor that received brief attention in the early sixties. In Vatican II's *Constitution of the Liturgy*, we read that "the rites and formulas for the sacrament of Penance are to be revised so that they give more luminous expression to both the nature and effect of the sacrament" (article 72). That such a directive can be given at all presupposes that the shape of the sacrament, as we have known it, fails to manifest its nature and effect in adequate fashion, that is, it does not meet the *Constitution's* demands.

Although the Holy See has not yet promulgated the revised forms of the sacrament of Penance, something can be done in the meantime—and is being done, within acceptable limits. What Paul says of the Spirit's work is true also of pastoral creativity: "There is no law against it" (Gal 5: 23). That creativity has manifested itself in the widespread phenomenon of "the communal celebration of the sacrament of Penance," also known as "communal, or group Penance." The very terms have scared some people; and ignorance of its nature and purpose (which are those of Penance itself!) has spawned many a rumor and false notion. Basically, the communal Penance is a modified bible service to prepare for the individual reception of the sacrament. It consists of scripture readings, homily, examination of conscience, individual confessions, imposition of a penance (private or group), absolution, and group thanksgiving. Such services can bring out the following themes: the social and ecclesial dimensions of sin, the reconciliation with God and the Church, the thanksgiving for the new life of grace. In addition to forming prudential attitudes and establishing a mature priority of values (through an adult examination of conscience), they can also provide instruction to those who come to confession only out of a sense of duty and encourage them to a deeper commitment. In other words, the communal Penance service can help the Christian community to repent and believe.

That is the purpose of the book. As with any worthwhile effort, it is the result of cooperation by many people, and they should be acknowledged for their generous sharing of talent:

The Liturgical Commission of the Archdiocese of New York, whose January 1971 *Bulletin* supplied material for the first three chapters;

The Coordinators of Religious Education of the Archdiocese of Baltimore, whose contributions make up the bulk of the suggested celebrations in chapter five;

Rev. Vincent Inghilterra, formerly of St. Mary's Seminary, Roland Park, Baltimore, who allowed the results of his personal study of the communal aspects of Penance to be incorporated as chapters seven and eight.

Rev. William Freburger
Executive Secretary,
Baltimore Archdiocesan Liturgical Commission

Chapter 1

Penance:
Scripture and Tradition

Charles Peguy once wrote: "The sinner and sin are one essential part of Christianity, a part on which Christianity hinges. The sinner is at the very heart of Christianity." The Bible presents us with the history of salvation, and, by that very fact, it presents us also with the history of man's sinfulness. The variety of Old Testament evidence helps us to understand sin as disobedience to God, unfaithfulness, rebellion, estrangement, a refusal to know God or to accept Him. The theology of the covenant in the Old Testament sees in sin more than individual perverseness, but a deed with calamitous social consequences. Sin is a universal reality affecting both the individual and the community. But the Old Testament also reveals God as one who delights in showing mercy, who continually calls back his erring people, who will love and forgive without limit. Finally, the Old Testament promises the forgiveness of a gracious God who will completely transform man and his community from death to life, "for with the Lord there is kindness, and plentiful redemption; it is He who will redeem Israel from all her iniquities" (Psalm 129).

The New Testament is the proclamation of the gospel, the good news of Jesus Christ as Savior. The proclamation of this

gospel of Christ "is the power of God unto salvation to everyone who believes" (Rom 1: 16). In the New Testament
proclamation we are faced with the preaching of Jesus, a
preaching concerned with sinful man: "I am come not to call
the just but sinners to repent" (Luke 5: 32). The repentance
or conversion *(metanoia)* to which the preaching of Jesus in-
sistently points is man's acceptance of God's forgiveness, and
of man's turning himself around to conform his way of life
to the standards and values of the Kingdom of God. This
teaching of Jesus reflects the joyful aspect in the acceptance
of the sinner who returns. This gospel of Jesus as Lord and
Messiah centers upon the death and resurrection of Jesus as
the once-for-all redeeming sacrifice. His blood is "poured
out for many for the forgiveness of sins" (Mt 26: 28). This
death of Christ "reconciles us with God" (Rom 5: 10; 2 Cor
5: 18), and opens for all men perfect access to God. The
centrality of the death and resurrection of Jesus in the New
Testament proclamation of God's decisive act in our favor is
proclaimed with insistency: "If Christ has not risen, vain is
your faith, for you are still in your sins" (1 Cor 15: 17).

As the New Testament focuses upon this decisive act of
God in history it also presents Baptism as the classic place for
the repentance of the individual and for the forgiveness of
sins. It is the new birth by the power of the Spirit into the life
of God's people. This activity of Baptism is completed and
perfected in the Eucharist because it is in Eucharist that the
event of Christ's death and resurrection is celebrated. Matthew's addition of "for the remission of sins" to the words
of the Lord, "This is my blood of the new covenant" indicates
a belief that after Baptism the Eucharist is the permanent presence of the deed of reconciliation in the covenant community.

However, we also find in Matthew's Gospel, "I tell you
solemnly, whatever you bind on earth is bound in heaven;
whatever you loose on earth is loosed in heaven" (18: 18).
And, in John's Gospel: "Receive the Holy Spirit. Those whose
sins you forgive, they are forgiven; those whose sins you
retain, they are retained" (19: 22-23). In this description of
these acts of the Church it is the Christian community which
designates the state of the sinner ("binding") who is not faithful to the life entered upon at Baptism. This is followed by the
Church's loosening; when the sinner fulfills the requirements

of the Church he can be restored to complete communion. In a real sense the Church "excommunicated" (not in our juridical sense) the sinner, that is, it excluded him from the Eucharist, *the* act of the Church; and, at the same time the Church "reconciled" a sinner to the community. So, for example, Paul's instructions in the 5th chapter of First Corinthians.

What emerges in this form of the tradition is that the Church of the New Testament also follows the Old Testament tradition of understanding sin as something which separated the sinner from God and also from his covenant-people. There exists a communal or social aspect not only regarding sin, but also regarding forgiveness. Sin not only offends God, it is a disruption of the community; penance and reconciliation affect the sinner before God, and also his relationship with the community.

The development of penance within the Church has a long and complex history. It involves many periods from which little or no information is available. It should always be remembered that simplistic presentations of the meaning of penance in the historical life of the Church are of their nature misleading, and definitive conclusions can be drawn only with great care.

In the age of the early Fathers we find evidence of the existence of post-baptismal sin, and of reconciliation with the community. We find no evidence for the details of uniform practice in the Church. The *Didache,* which reflects the Old Testament tradition of blessing and praising God, speaks of "confessing" one's sins in the Church; confession here is a public declaration of praise and glory to God and the admission of one's failures. Certainly the Church exercises some role for, as Poschmann reminds us, the Church is the community of salvation and "readmission into the Church is also a guarantee of God's forgiveness." In Tertullian we find evidence of a period of mortification and prayer before reconciliation to the Church and its Eucharist. Cyprian also witnesses a period of penance before reconciliation. These periods, it would seem, were for those who had committed only the gravest of sins; what is certain is that their terminus was reconciliation with the Church.

After Constantine, the new era of the Church and the great numbers who entered it led to some laxity; the severity of the older practices lessened the number who would undertake penitential discipline. Public penance was undertaken only once during one's lifetime; and this formal public reconciliation was sought only for grave sin. During this period, the place accorded Baptism continues to influence the development of penance: the significance of Baptism (as the definitive act of repentance) for a post-baptismal penance is reflected by Ambrose: "As there is only one Baptism there is only one penance." Penance came to be regarded as, and indeed was called, the "second Baptism." Its ritual paralleled that of Baptism: the catechumenate was mirrored by an "Order of Penitents."

This public order of penance seems to have had three steps:

(1) Confession of the sin(s) to the Bishop or priest who fixed the penance to be performed. This was an act of enrollment in the order of penitents.

(2) The actual performance of the penance laid down (prayer, mortification, abstinence, almsgiving, etc.).

(3) Public reconciliation after Lent. This reconciliation with the Church usually took place on Holy Thursday, so that those reconciled could celebrate the *triduum paschale*.

It is this communal aspect of penance which dominates what early evidence we have. The first witness to private penance is Canon 11 of the Third Synod of Toledo (589 A.D.), which condemns the practice as an abuse. In time, fewer and fewer participated in the public rites of penance, and it would seem we can find the movement towards a private reception beginning in Ireland (an area geographically isolated) as a pious practice arising from the religious life of monks, rather than penance as a liturgical celebration. By the tenth century the general practice of penance had lost much of its communal aspect: only priest and penitent are present, lesser sins are confessed, and the exercise of penance was done after and not before the reconciliation. During this period of transition penance came to be more and more a private affair, and ritual significance of its communal nature was limited to the fact that the ministry of the priest was necessary.

The developments in scholastic theology emphasized the juridical aspects of penance, and with it the temporal punishment due to sin. Confession, contrition and satisfaction were seen as the key elements, and the role of the Church was lessened (e.g. for Abelard the role of the Church in the sacrament is simply to supplicate). A stabilization of the theology of penance sets in with Thomas Aquinas; for him the matter of the sacrament embraced the acts of the penitent (confession, repentance, and satisfaction), and the form of the sacrament was the prayer of the priest (formula of absolution). The Council of Trent, reacting to reformation theology, taught the distinction of penance from Baptism, the necessity of the acts of the penitent (including confession of specific sins), the sufficiency of attrition, the necessity of the sacrament for mortal sins, and the priestly power of absolution. Poschmann summarizes the Tridentine definition as the affirmation of penance as (a) a sacrament, and (b) its being the efficient cause of the forgiveness of sins. He points to the ever-continuing and perplexing problem "of the relation of the subjective and personal factor to the objective and ecclesiastical one in the production of the forgiveness of sins."

Chapter 2

Penance:
The Present Situation

The most casual observer of Catholic life today cannot help noticing that the practice surrounding the sacrament of penance is less and less observed. An older generation of Catholics has been well trained in understanding the sacrament as distinct from the Eucharist, and in understanding a necessary relationship to Eucharist only in cases of grave sin. Today there is a growing tendency in religious education to prepare only for first communion and allow a later date for training in the demands of the sacrament of penance. In addition, after Vatican II, many found themselves dissatisfied with the "individualistic" aspects of penance, and have looked for a more social, or communal form for celebrating the sacrament.

In addition to these trends which surround penance, we must also face the realities of our time. A culture with a markedly decreasing sense of sin tends to give little credence to penance. The widening legalization of divorce, abortion, pornography, and drugs, coupled with the violence that pervades society demonstrates this diminishing sense of sin. It is no cause for wonder that our culture influences the understanding of sin and of the sacrament for the forgiveness of sin. But the influences are not all negative.

Since Trent Catholic theology and catechesis for the most

part devoted themselves to explaining and propounding the Tridentine doctrine. This presentation, coupled with the present liturgical form of the sacrament, continued to highlight the individualistic character of the sacrament—the sinner and his relationship with God. What is significant in the Church today is a concern for the social or ecclesial dimension of the sacrament. Developments in biblical studies, liturgical history, patrology and systematic theology have served to retrieve for the Church this fundamental corporate sense of the sacrament. By exposing the roots of the tradition, attention is focused upon the fact that the forgiveness of God is effected by reconciliation with the Church, the community of salvation, itself the sacrament of Christ. This sense of reconciliation, this objective ecclesial dimension, is not an extrinsic dimension or a simple juridical declaration; rather it is based upon the social nature of sin and the ecclesial nature of repentance.

The spirit of the second Vatican Council, with its emphasis upon the sacramental nature of the Church, did not end with the Council; indeed, it was strikingly reaffirmed by Pope Paul VI in the Apostolic Constitution, *Poenitemini*, in 1966. In that document the whole Church is called to restore to the world an authenticity and relevance in its ongoing proclamation of conversion and penance. One has only to be in contact with the documents of the Council, and the Church since the Council, to realize that the present thrust towards a more communal and Christian sense of penance *arises* from the authentic teaching of the Church.

However, it must also be stated that one would seriously err if he regarded this state of transition of the liturgical practice of the Church as one without problems. The first of these, which grows out of the complexities of the tradition which we have examined, is that of the individual confession of specific sins. To state that such confession is necessary, as some do, or to state as others do its "optional character," is to oversimplify and caricature some one element of the tradition and theology of the sacrament. It is evident that "confession" has always been a part of penance as received in the Church. Its forms have differed; the occasions of its necessity have differed. All theologians agree that confession in some sense is a necessary element; they differ on the individual specific or detailed confession. All would agree that *in the present discipline and practice* of the Roman Church it cannot be dispensed with except in very explicit and unusual circumstances (e.g. the soldiers about to enter battle, danger of self-exposure, etc.). There would be those who would go even further and feel that specific confession of sins is required by divine law.

General absolution without preceding auricular confession should not be confused with "communal sacramental absolution." General absolution is a technical, canonical term and has a specific definition. "Communal sacramental absolution" is, liturgically, a recent phenomenon. It occurs when one or several priests give absolution to several persons together after their individual confessions, each priest intending to absolve those persons who have confessed to him. There is no prohibition in canon law against this arrangement.

In accordance with paragraph 72 of the Constitution on the Sacred Liturgy, the Church is engaged in preparing reforms of the sacrament of penance. The first of these would be a reform of the rite and prayers of individual confession to bring out its ecclesial nature. Beyond this are proposals for a more communal celebration. The character of these reforms is to present the celebration of the sacrament in its joyful aspect as a celebration of the mystery of redemption. Sacramental reconciliation should express the evangelical teaching of the joy in heaven over the sinner who returns. This joyful characteristic is closely linked to the deliberate intent to restore the communal nature of the sacrament.

A "communal celebration" may be understood in a number of ways. One form has been in use in Europe since 1958 when it was first proposed at a liturgical study week in Vanves, France (whence it spread, in the early sixties, to Belgium, Italy, and Brazil). It has been described as "a celebration where Christians publicly confess before God and man that they are sinners; the priest invites them to this through a meditation on life and a request for the mercy of God on all of good will. In this celebration there is no specific confession of sins, nor is there the absolution which is given in private confession" (for a fuller treatment of this first form, cf. the appendix of this booklet).

Here in the United States, the "communal penance" that has developed over the past few years represents another form, involving hymns, readings, a homily, and prayers, within which provision is made for individual auricular confession. With this background, we can sketch the present possibilities for the pastoral ministry of penance:

1. *Individual specific confession.* This, of course, has been the usual form of the sacrament in our experience. Within the current situation, however, we must consider the following elements. Time: when is the sacrament available for the people? Attitude of the penitent: are catechesis and personal advice concerned with eliminating mechanistic conceptions of the sacrament? Attitudes of the confessor: does a business-like attitude continue to reinforce the mechanistic conception? Rite: does the confessor give the impression, in his ministry, that something magical is being uttered? Imposition of penance: is it an impersonal, mechanical "tax"?

2. *Public celebration of repentance.* This is the first communal form described above, not connected directly to the sacrament in any formal way. Its readings, songs, prayers and reflection emphasize the community's sense of the social dimensions of sin, and the communal responsibility to repentance and penance. In prior announcements and in the service itself, it should always be made clear to the people that this type of celebration is neither sacramental nor a substitute for the individual confession of serious sins. Any expression of the form of sacramental absolution should be avoided.

3. *Communal penance service.* This is the form most common here in the United States and is described at length in the rest of this booklet. This pattern is: a liturgy of the Word, individual confessions, concluding prayers of thanksgiving.

The spirit of renewal urges us to restore a sense of the Church community in the celebrations of the sacrament of penance. Priests must always make individual confessions attractive and forceful for the lives of the faithful. But, at the same time, through communal penance celebrations, we can reinforce our understanding of the social nature of sin, and of penance as a reconciliation with the Church.

Chapter 3

Guidelines for Parish Celebrations of Penance

These notes are intended as guidelines for parish celebrations of penance in common. They are culled from the experience of innumerable communities in the United States and around the world.

BEFORE THE CELEBRATION

Metanoia is a message. It is proclaimed: in the Gospels by John the Baptist; at the beginning of His ministry, by Jesus; on the first Pentecost by the Apostles. The proclamation of penance is a challenge and an invitation. There is a road to be travelled, because conversion is a process. The stages appear in the parable of the prodigal son, who first comes to his senses (*reflection*), then makes his *decision,* begins the return journey (*conversion*), at the end of which he makes his *confession* to his father and is *reconciled.* These stages are telescoped for the individual Christian as he prepares to confess during one of the weekly periods scheduled in any Catholic parish. Communal penance celebrations provide an opportunity for a full developing of this process. A number of parishes announce their penance celebrations weeks in advance, e.g. at the beginning of Lent for a celebration set in Holy Week. The announcement is issued as a proclamation, a call to penance to be achieved in the weeks ahead and ratified in the communal penance celebration.

The preparation would, naturally, involve a catechesis emphasizing conversion and reconciliation. A number of points could be made about the celebration itself. Obviously, the *communal and ecclesial* aspect of such a service needs some explanation. The note of *joy* should be evident; in the fifteenth chapter of Luke, "joy" (and its cognates) is the word most frequently used by Christ in the three parables on God's welcome to sinners. The *sacramental* dimension should also be emphasized—"sacramental" in that penance is an act of Christ and an effect of His paschal mystery.

COMPOSING THE SERVICE

1. *Choice of a theme.* This can be done according to the season (Lent, Advent Pentecost), occasion, or in response to a special need. A service on the occasion of the anniversary of the assassination of a public figure could focus on the theme "Violence in America; violence in ourselves." A special need in a parish which seems self-concerned and self-centered might prompt a service on "Keeping my brother." This is the most basic step in the preparation of the entire service, for all else depends on the theme. The theme determines the choice of materials for the rest of the service, and forms the basis of their formulation.

2. *Choice of readings.* This is done in accordance with the theme. The Scriptures are basic to this celebration, but other readings might be used in an auxiliary way to set the theme or provide reflection on the Scriptures. In the choice of Scriptures themselves, care must be exercised. For example, an Advent service should not concentrate on the necessity to prepare for the coming of the Lord to such an extent that it loses sight of the fact that he came and is present! The Scriptures have an integrity which must not be violated. The use of a book such as *Bible Themes* by T. Maertens will be helpful in achieving a balanced approach.

Some suggestions, readings of a general nature:

Ez 36: 25-31, "I shall give you a new heart." Note: omit verses 29 and 30.
Is 40: 1-5, "Prepare a way for our God."
Is 1: 15-18, "Wash and purify yourselves."

Mt 5: 1-10, "The beatitudes."
Mt 7: 21-27, "Put into practice the Word of God."
Eph 2: 13-18, "You who used to be so far apart have been
brought so close thanks to Christ."
I Jn 3: 10-18, "We know that we have passed from death
to life because we love our brothers."
Mt 25: 31-40, "I was hungry and you gave me to eat."
Lk 3: 2-14, "If anyone has two tunics he must share with
the man who has none." Note: omit verses 7-9.
Mt 7: 1-5, "Do not judge."
Mt 19: 16-22, "The rich young man."
Lk 15: 11-24, "The father of the prodigal son."
Lk 15: 25-32, "The elder brother of the prodigal son."
Lk 19: 1-10, "Zacchaeus."
Jn 8: 1-11, "The adulterous woman."
Rom 5: 6-11, "Freely saved by Christ."
I Cor 13: 1-7, "A hymn to charity."
Gal 5: 1-11, "Do not turn from liberty to slavery."
Eph 2: 1-9, "We were dead because of our sins, God
brought us to life in Christ."

3. *Examination of conscience.* Whereas the homily will be
both instruction and a call to conversion, the examination of
conscience should serve to personalize this conversion and
the call of God in our lives. It should be specific and a stimulus
to thought, an aid to reflection flowing directly from the
homily. In composing it, the aid of laymen who are familiar
with the way of life in the parish could be enlisted.

*Eight examples of examinations of conscience will be found at the end of
this chapter.*

4. *Auxiliary elements.* These are the prayers of opening
and closing, the hymns, periods of silence, litanies, responses,
meditations, etc. They should all support the major theme of
the celebration, and be chosen or composed in accordance
with it. They should be arranged around the readings, homily-
instruction, and examination of conscience. The number of
readings will help determine the choice and arrangement of
these elements. No celebration will have them all, or in the
same proportion as others. The *Our Father* is a good element
in a penitential service—not as a space-filler, but because of

its penitential nature (forgive us . . . as we forgive . . .). These elements, while secondary, are of great importance; a poverty of these elements will make the celebration too austere, an overabundance of them will obscure the major elements. Elements which are well-chosen and organic to the entire celebration will easily involve the entire community, whereas poorly chosen or disparate elements will be unable to build or sustain a spirit of penitence or an awareness of forgiveness. Expressions of human sinfulness, for example, should not be so graphic or overpowering as to destroy all sense of personal dignity or worth.

5. *Prepare a program with people's parts, and an indication of the elements of the celebration.* This sheet will enable the people to follow the celebration. It may contain words of explanation, but should not contain every text and word of the celebration—only people's parts.

DURING THE CELEBRATION

The atmosphere to be created during the service itself, by the celebrant and others, will necessarily take into account the varying approaches and responses, among the people, to confession, to penance, and to a public celebration of the sacrament. Those who will be experiencing the communal penance service for the first time may feel some anxiety and even confusion. There should be no hesitation in using specific and detailed comments in explanation.

The priests who serve as confessors may also need some direction and reassurance. There should be agreement beforehand about the method and meaning of the celebration. It might be well for a "master of ceremonies" or "leader" to brief the assembled clergy immediately before the service. He could stress the following points:

1. *This is a "concelebration"* of the sacrament of penance (in the same sense in which several priests or deacons concelebrate the sacrament of baptism, or "co-consecrators" concelebrate the sacrament of episcopal ordination). The main celebrant, then, would greet the congregation, lead the prayers, give the homily, and preside over the celebration. The concelebrants would hear the confessions and give absolution, in the form decided ahead of time (individually to each peni-

tent, or as "communal sacramental absolution"; cf. chapter two).

2. *It is important* that the participants appreciate the hierarchical nature of the assembly, for this is an ecclesial celebration. And yet, since it is a celebration of penance, it should also be apparent that there are no exceptions to the state of sin in the pilgrim Church. The group of confessors could very well manifest their own obedience to God's call to penance by confessing to each other before dispersing to hear the people's confessions. Obviously, there is no obligation for *each* priest to confess; the arrangement should be such that there is freedom in this regard.

3. *Obviously, the confessors* will not engage the penitents in lengthy dialogue. Questions would be kept to the necessary minimum, and any exhortation (except where necessary in a particular case) would be omitted since the homily of the main celebrant and the whole thrust of the celebration itself would supply for this. As with the method of absolution, a decision should be made ahead of time in regard to the "penance" imposed. Usually, the main celebrant will declare a penance for the assembled penitents after the confessions have been heard. In this case, any confessor is still free, of course, to impose a penance within the confession, especially in those cases where a general penance would be less beneficial than a particular one.

A number of directions should be given to facilitate the participation of the people:

1. *The freedom to go* or not go to confession depends on one's attitude or readiness. The people should be reminded that they may defer confession to another time. We can remind them of the times and dates scheduled for confessions.

2. *Method of confession:* Explain that since the preamble to the accusation itself has already been done communally, they can begin the accusation of their sins immediately. Remind the penitents that they are free to formulate the accusation of their sins in whatever way they want. Since one does not have to confess all his sins, except those of a grave nature, it is not necessary to tell everything. On the contrary, it would be more beneficial to make a confession that would be rep-

resentative of one's spiritual state and bearing on the points which would require a special marked effort following confession.

3. *Practical instructions* for choosing a confessor and for the reception of the sacrament itself. The penitents should be invited to meditation and thanksgiving before and after the individual confession.

4. *Sample explanatory text:* "Those wishing to receive the sacrament are invited to present themselves to one of the priests. The penitent will first confess any grave sin that may have been committed since his last confession and then other sins, especially those relating to the points emphasized during the common examination of conscience. After the priest has given absolution, the penitent answers: 'Amen.' (A common penance will be made before the end of the ceremony.) Everyone is invited to remember one of the points emphasized during the examination of conscience which would be the object of a particular personal effort at this time (season)."

These instructions may be given before confession. Certain points that are more important can be explained in the ceremony schedule which is handed out to the people before the penitential celebration. This will avoid too long an introduction, which is less effective.

SAMPLE EXAMINATIONS OF CONSCIENCE

Examination of conscience based on the virtues, the beatitudes, the commandments and the works of mercy can fittingly be made. These should be composed ahead of time by those making up the service. This is especially important when the public celebration is one associated with the sacrament of penance and includes auricular confession. The following examples of "thematic" examinations of conscience can also be used and are particularly fitting for communal celebrations of repentance. Other examples may be found in the services reprinted in the second half of this booklet.

Example 1. Choosing God.

Celebrant: Any constraint that you feel is in yourself. Open your minds the same way (2 Cor 6: 12). Become children of God (Jn 1: 12). Remain in the love of Christ (Jn 15: 9).

If somebody loves this world, the love of God is not in him (I Jn 2: 15-17). You are as unfaithful as adulterous wives; don't you realize that making this world your friend is making God your enemy? Clean your minds, you waverers (Jas 4: 4, 8).

—Have I decided to choose God? *(Silence)*

—Am I going to stop minimizing my obligations? *(Silence)*

—Have I decided to make of this Penance celebration a conversion, a change to a life more real, more open, more self-giving, and thus a happy life? *(Silence)*

"What the Spirit brings is very different: love, joy, peace, patience, kindness, goodness, trustfulness, gentleness, and self-control" (Gal 5: 22).

—Is my spiritual life broadly oriented, happy, overflowing? *(Silence)*

—Is it a life animated by the Spirit? *(Silence)*

Example 2. Life in faith.

Celebrant: "Do not model yourselves on the behaviors of the world around you, but let your behavior change, modelled by your new mind. This is the only way to discover the will of God and know what is good, what it is that God wants, what is the perfect thing to do" (Rom 12:2).

—Do I take time out to rectify my human judgments in the light of faith? *(Silence)*

—Am I, in my own life, consistent with my faith? *(Silence)*

Example 3. Apostolic duty.

Celebrant: "I, personally, am free . . . So though I am not a slave of any man I have made myself the slave of everyone so as to win as many as I could" (I Cor 9: 9, 19-23).

—Have I understood that apostolic dedication is strictly a "duty"? *(Silence)*

—As a member of (. . . . . organization), do I attend the meetings mainly for what I can get out of them for myself; do I try to bear witness to Christ and seek the glory of the kingdom? *(Silence)*

—If I am not a member of such organizations, do I feel relieved of all apostolic responsibility towards my "neighbor"? How do I relate with others? Do I consider them as human persons? Do I bear witness to Christ in my neighborhood? *(Silence after each question)*

Example 4. Sharing with others.

Celebrant: Blessed are you, Lord. By the words of John the Baptist you called us to conversion and contrition.

1st response: Pardon us for having been so indifferent.

2nd response: Pardon us for having made such a small effort to have a change of heart and to change our way of living. *(Silence)*

Celebrant: We hope in your mercy.

All: Lord have mercy on us.

Celebrant: Blessed are you Lord. By the words of John the Baptist you have shown us how to share with those who are in need.

1st response: Pardon us for having so often refused to share our time, our resources, and even our joy and friendship with others.

2nd response: Pardon us for so often allowing men, women and children of our country and other countries of the world to go hungry. *(Silence)*

Celebrant: We hope in your mercy.

All: Lord have mercy on us.

Celebrant: Blessed are you Lord. By your Son you wanted to come among men, to be close to them.

1st response: Pardon us for having so badly represented the presence of your love among men.

2nd response: Pardon us for having been so negligent in announcing your Good News to all men. *(Silence)*

Celebrant: We hope in your mercy.

All: Lord have mercy on us.

Celebrant: Blessed are you Lord. You gave us your Gospel, announcing the Good News of peace for all men.

1st response: Pardon us along with our generation for having worked so poorly in the remaking of a world wherein would reign peace and justice.

2nd response: Pardon us for our wars, our quarrels, our jealousies, and our selfishness. *(Silence)*

Celebrant: We hope in your mercy.

All: Lord have mercy on us.

Example 5. Greetings.

Celebrant: Treat each other in the same friendly way as Christ treated you (Rom 15: 7).

—Have I been able to welcome the other? Was I accessible? With my neighbors, did I try to overcome my timidity in order to make the first step? *(Silence)*

—Have I offered myself to others in times of necessity, anticipating their needs? *(Silence)*

Example 6. Superiority.

Celebrant: Treat everyone with equal kindness; never be condescending but make real friends with the poor. Do not allow yourself to become self-satisfied (Rom 12: 16).

—Do I give too much importance to the social status, to the external aspect, to what shows? *(Silence)*

—Have I tried sincerely to establish real relationships with people? Do I look for everyone as a person notwithstanding his social class, and thus not only as an employee, or worse, as an instrument? *(Silence)*

—Do I see in each man my own self? *(Silence)*

—Do I love each person, who is loved by Christ, as my brother? *(Silence)*

Example 7. Sharing.

Celebrant: Our love is not to be just words or mere talk, but something real and active (I Jn 3: 18). Behave like free men, and never use your freedom as an excuse for wickedness (Gal 5: 13). Serve ᴺe another in works of love (I Pt 2: 16). You should carry each other's troubles and fulfill the law of Christ (Gal 6: 2). Love is always patient and kind (I Cor 13: 4).

—Have I tried to serve, to spread joy in my environment? *(Silence)*

You received freely, give without charge (Mt 10: 8). I am testing the genuineness of your love against the keenness of others. Remember how the Lord Jesus was, . . . what we need is equality (2 Cor 8: 9). God loves those who give selflessly in joy (2 Cor 13: 11).

—Have I been generous? *(Silence)*

—Have I understood that I have an obligation to be generous since I have received much from God and from others? *(Silence)*

—How have I participated in the fight against hunger? *(Silence)*

—Does it often happen that I give to the community collection what I would be ashamed to give a poor man lest I make a mockery? *(Silence)*

Example 8. For children.

Happy the children who pray often and everywhere.

Do I think of the Lord and speak to God by praying to Him every day?

Do I sometimes praise and thank the Lord when I see all the beautiful things He has made and given to me?

Happy the child who uses the name of God respectfully.

Do I always speak of God with reverence?

Do I sometimes make fun of holy things?

Happy the child who keeps holy the day of the Lord.

Do I ever miss Mass on Sunday through my own fault?

Do I do my best to be on time for Mass on Sunday?

Do I do all I can to make Sunday a day of joy and rest for my family?

Happy the child who praises and gives thanks to the Lord.

Do I joyfully participate in the Mass by praying and singing with all my heart?

Do I intentionally tease or distract others in church by laughing, talking, or playing?

Happy the child who listens to God's words and obeys His commandments.

Do I do my best to listen closely to the Word of God during the readings and the sermon at Mass?

Do I go willingly to religion class so that I can learn to know and love the Lord better?

Do I pay attention to my parents and teachers when they talk to me about God?

Happy the child who loves and obeys his parents.

Do I sometimes thank God for giving me my parents who love me and take care of me?

Do I sometimes pray for my parents?

Do I thank my parents for all they do for me and give me?

(If there are parents present:

Happy the parent who loves his child.

Do I sometimes thank God for giving me my children?

Do I thank my children and my spouse for all the joy they have given me?

Do I pray for my children and my spouse?)

Happy the child who helps his parents and teachers, and tries to make them happy.

Do I help my parents do the work at home?

Do I obey my parents and teachers quickly and joyfully, and try to make them happy?

Do I thank my teachers for all they do for me?

Am I always loyal and respectful to my teachers?

Do I tell my parents and teachers I am sorry and ask them to forgive me?

Happy the child who is the friend to everybody.

Do I help and do things for my brothers and sisters, my classmates and other companions?

Am I always kind to everybody? Did I ever hit, kick or hurt others in any way? Do I play with everybody?

Am I careful not to keep anybody from playing with me on the playground?

Did I ever make fun or say mean things to those who are younger than I? Those of another race or religion? Do I always say "I'm sorry" when I'm at fault?

Happy the child who does his work with all his heart.

Do I try my best to do all my classwork and homework well?

Am I sometimes lazy or do I waste time by fooling around?

Can I stop watching TV and play and willingly go to bed on time so that I am able to work well the next day?

Happy the child who takes care of his body.

Do I enjoy gym and play games with all my heart?

Do I take care of my body and respect the bodies of others?

Happy the child who always tells the truth.

Do I always tell the truth to my parents and teachers?

Did I ever cheat in a class or game?

Did I ever steal or keep things that were not mine: money, toys, books?

Happy the child who feels, gives, and shares.

Am I always ready and happy to share my things with others?

Do I return things that I have borrowed?

Bibliography

P. Anciaux, *The Sacrament of Penance*. New York: Sheed & Ward, 1962.

C. Curran, "The Sacrament of Penance Today," *Contemporary Moral Problems*. Notre Dame: Fides, 1970 (= *id. Worship* 43 (1969) 510-531, 590-619; 44 (1970) 2-19).

B. Haring, *Shalom: Peace: The Sacrament of Reconciliation*. New York: Farrar, Straus & Giroux, 1967.

F. J. Heggen, *Confession and the Service of Penance*, University of Notre Dame Press, 1967.

J. Leclercq, "Confession and Praise of God," *Worship* 42 (1968) 169-176.

P. Palmer, *Sacraments and Forgiveness*. Sources of Christian Theology, 2. Westminster: Newman, 1959.

B. Poschmann, *Penance and the Anointing of the Sick*. New York: Herder and Herder, 1964.

J. Quinn, "The Lord's Supper and the Forgiveness of Sin," *Worship* 42 (1968) 281-291.

K. Rahner, "Forgotten Truths Concerning Penance," *Theological Investigations, II*. Baltimore: Helicon, 1963.

P. Schoonenberg, *Man and Sin*. Notre Dame: Univ. of Notre Dame Press, 1965.

A. von Speyr, *Confession, the Encounter with Christ in Penance*. New York: Herder and Herder, 1964.

Chapter 4

Preparation of Children
for Penance

The aim of this presentation is to deepen the children's understanding of the sacrament of Penance and to prepare them to enter into it in a meaningful way. In preparation for this presentation, the children should bring to class pictures which they feel express attitudes contained in the word, "penance." Among such attitudes would be included: sorrow, forgiveness, peace, love, selfishness, repentance, etc. The class should spend some time discussing the ideas these pictures engender. At that point, the teacher can begin to present the following:

Can you think of any occasion where Christ speaks of penance or repentance? Recall Matthew 3: 17.

"Repent, for the kingdom of heaven is close at hand." Why do you think Christ related repentance with the kingdom of heaven? The kingdom of God is a way of living that is filled with the care Christ has for others. To live in the kingdom is, first of all, something on the inside. It means one loves more. The kingdom of heaven is already present when Christ's love is active in someone. To repent then means to change one's ways of living. It may mean turning away from sin. It always means turning more toward God. This is why Christ was always concerned with leading people to repentance—it was part of bringing them to His Father's love. Can you recall some of the people whom Christ forgave? (Mary Magdalen, Zaccheus, the paralytic, the good thief.)

Christ's heart was so filled with the desire to tell us of the Father's love and His desire to forgive us that He gives us a beautiful story of a boy who needs forgiveness. We call this boy the "prodigal son" or "lost son."

The boy is very selfish. We will put him in a circle because he is unable to think of anyone but himself. To show how much he thinks about himself, Jesus tells us that one day he goes to his father and says, "Let me have my share of the family money." Is there anything wrong with this? (Let students discuss.) It does seem very greedy to want his money all at once. And Jesus tells us that he is greedy, for he goes to a faraway country, and spends it all on fun and good times for himself. He doesn't ask, "How much can I help some poor person who doesn't have any money at all?" He doesn't think about sharing with needy people.

What about the poor father? How many times he wonders how he can get his boy back home with him again! Of course, the boy has to make that decision himself. He has to come to his senses and see that he has really hurt his father.

Something happens which helps the boy think about what he has done. The country where he had so much fun for himself is in famine. Do you know what that means? Yes, they are out of food and money. What will he do now? He'll have to get a job. Even that is not easy to do. He finally finds a job working on a farm feeding pigs. Even the pigs have more and better food than he. He begins to think. (Show a picture of the boy in this dejected state. Discuss the thoughts and feelings of the boy.)

Jesus tells us that something is beginning to happen. He sees what a good father he has. How could he have left him? How could he have been so unloving? Even his father's servants are happier than he because they are doing what his father wants. He makes a decision. He is not going to be that selfish boy any longer. He is going back to his father and tell him he is sorry for leaving him. He loves his father. But will his father take him back?

Let's look back home. See the father is looking out in the

distance. He sees a poor, bedraggled boy coming down the road. He recognizes his son. Look he goes out to meet him with open arms. He loves the boy. He is ready to forgive. The boy is trying to say, "Father, forgive me for I have sinned." All the father can think of is how happy he is to have his son back again. He calls his servants to prepare for a party. His son who was lost is found. He wants to celebrate.

What do you think Jesus is telling us in this story? (Discuss the idea of the father showing the great love and compassion of God for us, the disposition of the son before and after his change of heart, etc. Some of the following material may come out of the discussion.)

Jesus knows that we need a way to come back to our Father when we have not loved as much as we should. He gives us a sign of forgiveness in the priest who takes his place. We call this the Sacrament of Penance, or the Sacrament of Forgiveness. For those who have turned away from our Father's love completely, for those who have really rejected God, i.e., those in serious sin, this sacrament is a means of returning to Him. For those who have not separated themselves from Him completely, but have been weak and selfish and have not loved as much as they could, the Sacrament of Penance is a means of telling Jesus they want to love Him more. The priest can help and direct us to grow in love of Jesus. It is the Sacrament of PEACE and happiness. Jesus wanted to be able to bring this peace and happiness to everyone, not just those who were living in Palestine with Him. This is why Jesus said on Easter Sunday to his priests:

> "Peace be with you. 'As the Father sent me, I am sending you.' Receive the Holy Spirit; whose sins you forgive, they are forgiven; whose sins you retain, they are retained."

More than anything else our Father wants us to be sorry for our selfishness. He looks to our heart more than to the words we say. He wants to see love there. He wants to see that we want to try to do better. Before we go to confession, we look back over our lives. We remember some of the good, kind things that we have done, but sometimes we see selfishness. We have to ask ourselves why did I act that way. (Help the children to really analyze the deeper causes; work at the root of the problem.)

The way in which we ask forgiveness is by telling the priest in our own words that we have done what was not pleasing to God. If we wish, as we begin our confession, we can ask Father for forgiveness. We may want to tell him our name or how long it has been since we confessed to a priest. After we have talked to him about the ways in which we were unloving, we should tell him we are sorry and will try to do better. Sometimes Father will be able to help us see what needs to be done.

Then Father will give us a penance. This is a sign of our desire to make up for our selfishness and enter into a deeper friendship with God and those persons whom we may have hurt. Sometimes the priest asks us to help decide what would be a good way to make up for the particular sins or faults we have mentioned. (Students might discuss what would be appropriate penances for various acts of selfishness.)

Then Father says the words which tell us that Jesus is forgiving us. Listen closely:

> May Our Lord Jesus Christ absolve you, and by His authority I absolve you from your sins, in the name of the Father and of the Son and of the Holy Spirit.

He blesses us with the sign of the Cross as he says these words of forgiveness to remind us that it is through the loving self-giving of Jesus in his death and resurrection that we are united in love to the Father.

The lost son must have felt many wonderful things in his heart when he came back to his father. What do you imagine he said to his father? He must have said "thank you" many times. Don't you think we have much for which to say "thank you" to Father who takes Jesus' place? Perhaps even now we could have a moment of thanks to Jesus for giving us the wonderful sacrament of forgiveness.

Activities

1. Dramatize the Prodigal son with a Scripture reading. One child can take the part of the narrator, one the part of the father, and one the part of the son. The son should leave the father at the appropriate reading and make the return to give the sense of turning away from the father, and turning back to him.

2. Role play a contemporary "lost son," i.e., a father telling his son to do some chores around the house. The son goes off to a movie, but becomes sorry and comes home to the father with an apology and promise to do extra chores.

3. Do the four classroom themes as suggested by Father Anthony Bullen in "When First Confession is Delayed," reprint from The Catechist, vol. 3, no. 1, Sept. 1969.

4. Have each child make a collage contrasting selfishness in the world on the one side with loving actions on the other side. Discuss that the loving actions can be ways of doing penance for the lack of love that exists in the world.

5. Plan for a classroom "Penance Celebration."

6. Plan a Sacramental Celebration of Penance in which the children are joined with their parents.

Chapter 5

Celebrations of Penance for Various Age Levels

PRIMARY GRADES

The children gather at the feet of the priest or the teacher, who sits in a chair in front of them.

Teacher: You know, Jesus loved to have children and grown-ups gather around Him and they were always doing it because He was so nice and kind and they liked to be near Him. He had so many things to teach them about. Sometimes He told them interesting stories and sometimes He just talked to them.

One time, He told them this—now remember: this is Jesus talking to you, so shut your eyes a minute and imagine you are on a green hillside and it is really Jesus you are sitting in front of. This is what He says:

Someday I will come to you and say: you have shared and been very loving. When I was hungry you gave me food When I was thirsty you gave me water. When I was a stranger you brought me home. When I had no clothes you gave me some. When I was sick you took care of me. When I was in prison you visited me. And you will say to me: When did we see you hungry and feed you, thirsty and give you drink? When did we see you a stranger and bring you home or without clothes and gave you some or in prison and visited you? When? And I will say: Believe me, when you did it to one of the least of my brethren, you did it to me.

And then I will say to some: You have *not* shared and loved. (Repeat negative of above paragraph). Then, believe me: when you *refused* these things to the least of my brethren, you refused it to me.

There follows a brief discussion with the children concerning the meaning. Then, all stand, form a circle holding hands, and sing an appropriate song (e.g., "Whatsoever You Do").

Teacher: All of us belong to God's family. God the Father is *our* Father. The Lord Jesus is *our* brother. His Holy Spirit lives within *us*. All of us are united to each other in this family.

The teacher then invites the children to name activities that destroy this family unity. The teacher demonstrates by dropping the hands of his neighbors, stepping into the circle, and speaking, then moving back when finished.

Teacher: But sometimes we hurt one another when we are selfish and want our own way.

Child #1: We hurt our parents when we disobey them.

Child #2: We hurt our brothers and sisters when we fight with them.

Child #3: We hurt anyone when we make fun of them.

One of the children, prepared beforehand, then steps into the circle and reads the following:

Reader: When we understand that some things we do hurt others we are sorry because we don't want our friends and family to be unhappy. And when we see we have made them unhappy we want to tell them we are sorry and have them forgive us. We want everything to be all right again and we know that when people forgive us things are nice between us again.

Teacher: Since we have just learned that doing something to others is like doing it to Jesus we want to ask His forgiveness. Just as He loves to have children come to be near Him, so He is always waiting with His arms out for us to be friends again when we are sorry for doing something we shouldn't have. He is always waiting to forgive us when we come running back to Him because we are sorry.

Let's think quietly for a moment to see if we have remembered some important things Jesus wants us to do.

After a few moments of silence, a number of children step into the circle, one-by-one, and read the following from slips of paper prepared ahead of time:

Child #1: Am I kind to my parents and all adults?

Child #2: Am I kind to my brothers and sisters?

Child #3: Am I kind to my friends?

Child #4: Am I kind to those who are unkind to me?

Child #5: Do I help people who need help? Even my brothers and sisters?

Child #6: Do I forgive people who hurt me?

Child #7: Am I always truthful?

Child #8: Do I think of Jesus and talk to Him every day so that we can become better friends?

All the children form a circle again, but without holding hands.

All: We are sorry, Lord, if we haven't done some of these things. We will ask those we have hurt to forgive us. We ask You, Lord Jesus, to forgive us. We want to be friends again.

Teacher: Close your eyes and think of Jesus and his loving forgiveness. (Pause for a few moments.) Open your eyes now and join your hands again.

The service concludes with a rousing hymn, e.g. "Shout From The Highest Mountain."

SIXTH GRADE

This penitential celebration was originally composed for a sixth-grade C.C.D. class. It may, of course, be used with other groups on that age level.

Leader: May the peace of the Lord be with you.

Class: And also with you.

Leader: The Lord Jesus Christ invites you to come and see yourselves as you really are, as children of God and friends of each other. All of us, in one way or another, have been selfish. We have sinned against God and each other. But Jesus loves us and wants to free us from our sins. Let us draw near his altar.

The Leader invites the class to the altar. The children stand around it.

Leader: This altar reminds us of the gift Jesus has given of himself. He calls us into his Church, shelters us, and protects us. He feeds us with his body and blood, and gives us persons to guide and help us: fathers and mothers, priests and sisters, teachers and friends. Jesus speaks to us through them, and also through the book of his Word. How many gifts he has given us! He has made us rich. Hold hands now as we make a circle around the altar. Look at one another. See, we are not alone; God has called us together. God loves each one of us. He wants us to know that each one of us is important and has special gifts. God our Father and Jesus our Brother asks us to love and treat others as members of the family. By calling us together to be members of his Church, Jesus frees us from loneliness, poverty, ignorance, and prejudice. He asks us to help others so that we may be free from selfishness. Now let us ask forgiveness for the times we have willingly done wrong to others.

The group reflects in silence, then engages in the following litany:

Leader: For the times we refused to be friendly to those who are lonely:

Class: We are sorry, Lord.

Leader: For the times we said mean things about others or to others:

Class: We are sorry, Lord.

Leader: For the times we stole or spoiled what belongs to others:

Class: We are sorry, Lord.

Leader: For the times we refused to share our things or our friendship:

Class: We are sorry, Lord.

Leader: For the times we were selfish.

Class: We are sorry, Lord.

Leader: Let us tell God how sorry we are. Repeat each sentence after me:

O my God, I have sinned . . .
I disobeyed you and hurt others . . .
I deserve to be punished . . .
I am sorry, Lord, forgive me . . .
I know you love me . . .
And I want to love you more . . .
I firmly resolve with Jesus' help . . .

After an appropriate song, the leader says:

Leader: Now we go to confession to get God's help to lead a new and better life. We will return with renewed strength to grow up as Christians. While we wait our turn, we will pray.

Let us pray for our friends who are confessing their sins: "Lord Jesus, give them strength." (Children repeat)

Let us pray for all the people who are lonely and rejected: "Lord Jesus, give them comfort." (Children repeat)

Let us pray for all the people in the world: "Lord Jesus, teach us to help." (Children repeat)

Let us thank Christ our Savior for the sacrament of peace and freedom: "Lord, we thank You for the gift of peace." (Children repeat)

And similar petitions may be added, as many as necessary. The service then concludes with a hymn of thanksgiving.

EIGHTH GRADE—CHRISTMAS

After an opening hymn, the priest greets the group of students and leads them in an opening prayer. He briefly explains the purpose of the celebration, and then introduces the first reading.

First Reading: Luke 15: 11-32 (Prodigal Son)

After an appropriate response, the second reading is introduced.

Second Reading: Luke 2: 1-12 (Magi)

Again, an appropriate response; then, the celebrant gives the homily. There follows the preparation for confession.

Priest: Lord Jesus Christ, we come to confess our sins.

Students: We come with anxiety and sorrow, with hope and expectation.

Priest: We come to Bethlehem, seeking the Christ child.

Students: We see you in the stable, lying in the manger. You were deserted because we had no room in our hearts.

Priest: Lord Jesus Christ, we come to adore You and ask Your forgiveness.

Students: As we gaze upon You, we are suddenly ashamed of all our wrongdoing.

Priest: Lord Jesus, when we kneel down beside You—

Students: We remember how we treated our parents, our friends, our neighbors, our God, and we feel sorry for our negligence.

Priest: Lord Jesus Christ, while we are kneeling beside You—

Students: We see a clear image of our wrongdoing. We see a hungry world before us, the pain of starving children, the guilt of war, the terror of people without rights, and we know that we share in these evils.

Priest: Lord Jesus Christ, when we come to Bethlehem—

Students: We cannot escape what we are: lonely and greedy, caught in selfish love.

Priest: Lord Jesus Christ, we face You now as never before, as the forgotten and pushed aside, as the newborn Savior.

We have come to You today—

Students: To confess our guilt, our pain, our emptiness . . .
to look for hope from You.

During the hearing of individual confessions, Christmas carols may provide a meditative background—especially the carols that emphasize the Savior's coming to liberate man from sin. After the confessions, the litany of thanksgiving is said:

Priest: Men of God, why have you come to see the newborn?

Students: Because we are afraid, we are uncertain, we are uncomfortable here, and we have doubts about this child.

Priest: Do not be afraid for the Savior has been born to us. He is among us now to save us from our faults. Men of God, why are you here?

Students: Because we feel guilty, we feel lonely, we feel lost, for we deserted this newborn baby.

Priest: Do not feel guilty any longer, for He has humbled Himself to become one of us, and He is here among us now.

Students: We rejoice at the sight of our Savior. We ask His forgiveness. We are joyful.

Priest: Men of God, the Savior is in your midst.

Students: Yes, He has been born among men.

Priest: He has promised you He would come.

Students: And He is here.

Priest: Alleluia.

Students: Alleluia.

Priest: He is our Savior.

Students: And He is here.

The service concludes with a hymn and a dismissal.

JUNIOR HIGH

In addition to the priest, the entrance procession includes: students bearing cross, candles, Bible, stoles, and banners; five student readers. The readers are seated near the lectern.

Reader #1: We have come here today to celebrate publicly the mercy and forgiveness of our heavenly Father. When we realize that we have weakened our relationship of love with God, we are really sad. When we realize that this relationship can be made new and strengthened by sorrow and penance, we are glad indeed. A celebration is called for.

As an opening to our celebration, (Name: reader #2) will offer a few introductory remarks.

Reader #2: When God created us, He made us to His image. No other blessing of His is more significant than that. Being made to His image, we are set apart above the rest of the creatures of the earth. Being made to His image, we are empowered to love. It is by loving that we grow ever more in the likeness of our God. Nonetheless, we must admit that as humans we are weak. At Baptism, we are in a state of love and innocence, but it is not long before we experience the sin in our world. Sooner or later, we sin too; that is, we fail to love our fellowman, we fail to love ourselves, we fail to love God. Yet we find that people can be good: in time they do forgive those who have hurt them. This forgiveness of our fellowman is a reflection of the forgiveness of God. He, most of all, in His majesty and glory, is kind and merciful, loving and forgiving. This mercy, this forgiveness we celebrate today.

Reader #1: As an expression of our trust in the mercy of God, (Name: reader #3) will lead us in a prayer from the Old Testament Book of Sirach. Please kneel.

Reader #3: You who fear the Lord, wait for his mercy.

Students: Do not turn aside in case you fall.

Reader #3: You who fear the Lord, trust him.

Students: And your reward will not be lost.

Reader #3: You who fear the Lord, hope for good things.

Students: Hope for everlasting happiness and mercy.

Reader #3: For the Lord is tender and merciful.

Students: He forgives sins, he saves in time of trouble.

Reader #3: Those who fear the Lord do their best to please him.

Students: And those who love him keep his ways.

Reader #3: Those who fear the Lord keep their hearts ready.

Students: And humble themselves in his presence.

Reader #1: In humility, in confidence,
let us call on the Lord.

Students: Lord, have mercy on us.
Christ, have mercy on us.
Lord, have mercy on us. *(Each three times)*

Reader #1: When a sinner has said that he is sorry and is ready to love again, God our Father forgives him. In a few short words, our savior Jesus Christ gave us the sacrament of Penance. In this sacrament, in sorrow and confession, we publicly celebrate this return to the Father. At the same time, we celebrate our return to the community of believers, the People of God.
(Name: reader #4) will read to us the words of Jesus. Please stand.

Reader #4: This reading is taken from the Gospel of St. John, chapter 19, verses 19-23.

Students: (At the end of the reading) Thanks be to God.

The priest then gives a homily to explain the Scripture and the celebration. There follows an examination of conscience. The examination may be composed in any one of the following ways:

1) the students write their own prior to the celebration;

2) a choice is made from the usual examinations found in manuals of prayer;

3) a selection is made from the various lists contained in other services in this booklet.

Student reader #5 takes his place at the lectern and leads the others in the examination. He pauses momentarily after the mention of each item.
After the examination, individual confessions are heard. The service concludes with the exchange of the sign of peace and the singing of an appropriate hymn.

GENERAL PENANCE SERVICE—I

The service may be used in any liturgical season. After the opening hymn, the celebrant says the following prayer while all kneel:

Priest: Father in heaven, we come together to confess our sins. We come with deep confidence that, as we prepare together, we will see more clearly your great concern for us, so that when we come to meet your Son in confession, we will be open to that meeting and will obtain forgiveness through him whose love for us lasts for ever and ever.

People: Amen.

If desired, the Teleketics' film, Penance: Sacrament of Reconciliation, may be shown in conjunction with the reading from Scripture, Luke 15: 11-24. After the reading, an appropriate song or recited response is followed by the homily. Then, priest and people together say:

Lord, forgive us the lack of love in our lives;
forgive us as you always forgave those close to you.
Help us today and every day
to live in your presence
so that we may be reminders of you
to those around us.
Give us the strength
to love until it hurts
and then to keep loving
so that we may be one
even as you, your Son, and the Spirit are one.

All are seated for the examination of conscience on attitudes.

Priest: Sin is not only a breaking of the law; it is a way of life. Let us look at the way we live; let us examine our attitudes and outlooks. I am sorry for making things or money or people more important than God. I am sorry for not taking sufficient time to pray, for not making prayer a family activity. I am sorry for being listless at Mass. I am sorry for a shallow sense of faith.

I am sorry for not making time to understand the Scriptures better, for not searching out the reasons for the changes in the Church.

I am sorry for not being serious about Lent.
I am sorry for not loving the Church even while I criticize her.
I am sorry for not growing in hope in the midst of a despairing world.
I am sorry for taking people for granted, especially members of my own family. I am sorry for not trying to make them happy.
I am sorry for not forgiving someone when they rub me the wrong way. I am sorry for getting even with people by not talking to them.
I am sorry for not working with the responsibility expected of me.
I am sorry for not putting in the full day that I get paid for.
I am sorry for not trying to become more competent in my field.
I am sorry for trying to be important in front of my friends.
I am sorry for pulling others down so as to elevate myself.
I am sorry for hating people who are different; I am sorry for not caring about others. I am sorry for the greed and misery that make me want so many useless things.
I am sorry for feeling sorry for myself.

All: Father, all that I have, you have given me.
Your Son, Jesus Christ died to give me new life.
I am sorry for having refused your gifts.
I ask you to give me another chance.
Help me to fight the good fight,
to run the race as a true believer,
and to gain the prize that you have prepared
for all those who persevere in the faith.

After a few moments of silent reflection, the celebrant commissions the confessors:

Priest: Our Lord has said: "Peace be with you. As the Father sent me, so I am sending you. Receive the Holy Spirit. For those whose sins you forgive, they are forgiven." Therefore, my brother priests, for those who come to you asking forgiveness, forgive in the name of Jesus.

During the individual confessions, the following readings, interspersed with song, may provide appropriate meditation: Daniel 9: 3-7, Joel 2: 12-13; Psalm 32. After confessions, all recite the following:

All: Lord, grant that I may avoid useless attacks
that tire and wound without achieving results.
Keep me from those angry outbursts
that draw attention but leave me weakened.
Keep me from wanting always, in my conceit,
to outstrip others, crushing those in my way.
Wipe from my face the sullen look of self-pity.
Lord, grant that I may live my days calmly and fully.
Make me deep like the sea
and let me spread your influence
like the water that covers the whole shore.
May I wait for my brothers
and match my pace to theirs
that I may move forward together with them.
May each of my retreats turn into an advance.
Illumine my life so that I may sing and dance
with the triumphant radiance of your joy.
May all those who draw near me
go away refreshed, eager to live and love forever.

At this point, the greeting of peace may be exchanged as an action-comment to the preceding prayer. Then the celebrant gives the final blessing:

Priest: You are God's chosen race. He loves you and you should be clothed in sincere compassion, in kindness and humility, gentleness and patience. Bear with one another; forgive each other as soon as a quarrel starts. The Lord has forgiven you: now you must do the same to your brother. Put on love and the peace of Christ will reign in your hearts. Be merciful and always be thankful. May God bless you and keep you. May God uncover his face to you and bring you peace. Amen.

The service concludes with a hymn of thanks and praise.

GENERAL PENANCE SERVICE—II

This service may be used in any liturgical season. After the entrance hymn, the celebrant begins:

Priest: The Lord be with you.

People: And also with you.

Priest: Let us pray. (Pause)

>Our Father, we stand before you as men,
>and also as your children—in need of you.
>You have chosen us,
>and given us the wonders of human life.
>You have loved us forever,
>and shared with us your divine life.
>And yet, we know we are still human:
>we acknowledge our sin,
>our sickening selfishness,
>our refusal to love and to give.
>We beg you now
>to forgive us,
>to give us new life,
>to free us from all in our lives
>that is less than human and Christian.
>We beg forgiveness from all our brothers
>whom we have used, with whom we have not shared
>our love.
>Our Father, restore us to life,
>make us new,
>make all things new,
>through Jesus Christ, your Son, our Lord.

People: Amen.

The Scripture reading is Matthew 5: 1-16. After the reading, the people make the following response:

People: Lord Jesus Christ, we give you thanks
>that you have come to call sinners.
>You forgive our guilt
>and invite us to share the banquet of the Eucharist.
>For it is in the breaking of the bread
>that we recognize your presence.

It is in the drinking of the cup of your blood
poured out for the forgiveness of sins,
that we find reconciliation with you
and with all our brothers and sisters.

The homily is followed by a period of silent reflection on one's sinfulness. The litany for pardon closes the reflection:

Priest: If we say we have no sin, we deceive ourselves and the truth is not in us.

People: Hear, O Lord, and grant pardon.

Priest: With Peter the Apostle, we say: Depart from me, Lord, for I am a sinful man.

People: Hear, O Lord, and grant pardon.

Priest: Mindful of Mary Magdalen and the thief on the cross, we come to you in confidence.

People: Hear, O Lord, and grant pardon.

Priest: You, O Christ, remain our advocate, to plead our cause before the Father.

People: Hear, O Lord, and grant pardon.

Priest: You, O Lord, the Most Holy, have taken our sins upon yourself and bore them in your body on the cross.

People: Hear, O Lord, and grant pardon.

Priest: O God, you desire the repentance of the sinner and not his death. Take into consideration our frail human nature. Be merciful to us, for you know that we are dust. Forgive us and grant us the peace you have promised to sincere penitents. Through Christ our Lord.

People: Amen.

Priest: We have spoken of our sinfulness and of our desire to be forgiven. Let us now make those words into a sign, to one another and to the Lord: a sign filled with the Spirit, a sign of the Lord's presence to his people, a sign of his working in our midst, his sign that is the sacrament of penance. The confessors will be located. . . .

Appropriate hymns are sung during the private confessions. When all confessions have been heard and the celebrant returns to the altar:

Priest: Lord Jesus Christ, in this sign you are with us; your mercy washes us; we are your people. May this sign be a source of life for us. May your Spirit lead us in this world. We make this prayer through you who live with the Father and the Spirit as our God, for ever and ever.

People: Amen.

Priest: Now, let us show that we are at peace with God and with one another. Let us offer each other a sign of peace.

Once the sign has been exchanged, the service concludes with a hymn of thanksgiving.

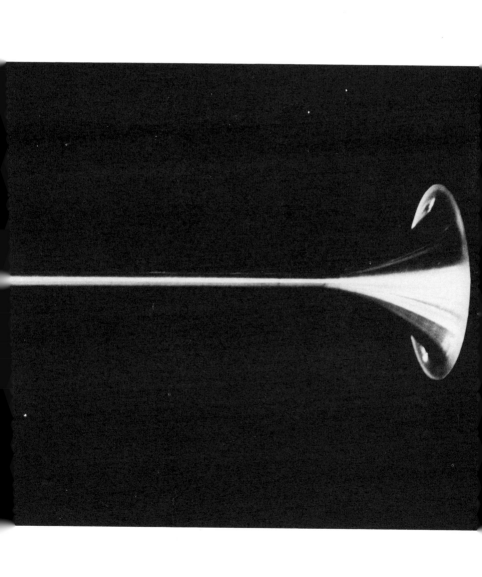

Chapter 6

Lenten Penitential Programs

INTRODUCTION

In its earliest beginnings, sometime before the fourth century, the "season" of Lent consisted of three Sundays which at the time constituted the sole preparation for Easter. This preparation was dominated by three important Scripture passages, all of them from the Gospel of John, proclaimed each in turn on the Sundays during the approach to Easter: John 4 (the Samaritan woman at the well), John 9 (the man born blind), John 11 (the raising of Lazarus). By the end of the fourth century, the catechumenate—the preparation of adult converts for Baptism at the Easter Vigil—had to some extent taken over these readings, so rich in baptismal symbols (water, light, risen life), and was using them directly for the preparation for Baptism. During the sixth century, infant baptism took the place of the baptisms for adults, and these readings, and their related ceremonies, were moved from the Sundays of Lent to the weekdays, where they remained until the liturgical revisions initiated by Vatican II. *The New Lectionary for Mass*, issued in 1969 and now in use, assigns these readings to the last Sundays of Lent in the first year of the three-year cycle of readings, and urges that they be used also in the other two years.

This restoration, as well as the revised rites for Holy Week, guarantee the desire of Vatican II that, in Lent, "the baptismal and penitential themes should be more pronounced" (*Constitution on the Liturgy,* no. 109). It is now imperative that our appreciation of Lent move beyond the level of "practices of self-denial" and take on the broader scope indicated by the liturgical reform. The "baptismal and penitential" nature of Lent is for *everyone,* both the to-be-baptized and the already-baptized. During this season, the whole Church lives again the mystery of conversion and initiation. Even the baptized need conversion, a "change of heart" achieved in that Sacrament which has been called a "second Baptism"— the Sacrament of Penance. For these reasons, then, Lent begins each year under the sign of conversion. In addition to the traditional formula accompanying the imposition of ashes ("Remember, man, that you are dust," etc.), the priest may use Christ's challenging invitation from Mark's Gospel: "Repent, and believe the Good News!" Repent—that is, change your heart, be converted.

The Lenten program presented here has, as its first purpose, an appreciation of conversion, the purpose of Lent itself. The third session, suggested for the Wednesday of Holy Week, is a Communal Penance service, based on the theme of light and employing the motifs of John's eleventh chapter (the man born blind). This corporate, collective act of conversion is the fitting conclusion of the previous two sessions, based respectively on the symbols of water and of life as exemplified in the readings from John 4 and 11.

The second purpose of this program centers on the liturgical symbolism itself. There is a growing concern that the recent reform in the Church has destroyed the rich symbolism of our liturgy, that the ritual "density" so characteristic heretofore of the Roman Catholic Church has now been replaced by the lean phrasings of a bland vernacular and the impoverished ceremonies of an eviscerated liturgy. This concern is legitimate. It is well-founded, as Maertens and Frisque point out in their consideration of the status of water symbolism in our day:

> *For modern man, water has lost its sacral value—at least apparently, for its fundamental symbolism has undoubtedly taken refuge in the profound zones of*

*his consciousness, where it continues to play an
equivalent role. In any case, water appears today
above all in its profane significance; modern man
has need for water like his predecessors, but he is
learning better and better how to domesticate this
natural element. Under these conditions, can water
still serve as a vehicle for the message of salvation?
Has not modern man become a stranger to the symbolism of water used by the liturgy of the catechu-
mens and the ritual of baptism?*

The Belgian liturgists do not despair; they quickly add,
"In reality, these questions posed by modern man, far from
ruining the sacramental symbolism of water, are an invitation
to arrive at a more profound understanding of its specifically
Christian character." They cite, in particular, the passage
from John 4 as a starting point for this "more profound understanding" of the water symbolism in Christianity. If this
program seems unduly centered on the symbols involved in
the traditional texts from John's Gospel, it is due to the desire
to promote the meaning and place of this symbolism in the
life of baptized Christians in need of conversion (that is, in
the lives of us all).

FIRST SESSION: FOURTH WEEK OF LENT

In emphasizing the symbol of water, this first session in-
tends to place the process of Lenten conversion in perspective
for those who participate. Their need of conversion does not
exist in a vacuum; they have been baptized. This initial celebration recalls very explicitly the use of water in Baptism and
links it with the living faith that is at the heart of conversion
("Repent, and believe!"). If the church contains a baptismal
font located in or near the sanctuary, it is filled with water
and serves as the focal point of the celebration. If the font
is not at hand to the sanctuary, an appropriate basin is placed
on a table in view of all.

*As the service begins, the priest and ministers enter in procession as the
congregation sings a hymn expressive of the theme of the celebration. The
priest then speaks the following prayer:*

My brothers and sisters, you have been taught that

when we were baptized in Christ Jesus we were baptized in His death—in other words, when we were
baptized, we went into the tomb with Christ and
joined Him in death. Our former selves have been
crucified with Him to free us from the slavery of sin.
If you are dead to sin, how can you continue to live
in it?

Let us pray that our celebration this evening may lead
us to return to the way of life which we began in
our Baptism.

(Pause for silent prayer)

God our Father, in the waters of Baptism, we imitated
Your Son Jesus Christ in His death. Now we desire
to return to life with Him.
Death has no power over Him anymore. When He
died, He died once for all to sin. Help us in this
Lenten season, Father, to share the life that He now
lives with You, in the unity of the Holy Spirit, for
ever and ever.

*All are seated and the lector introduces the reading, John 4: 5-42. The text
may be found in the New Lectionary for Mass, in a longer or shorter version,
under number 28-A (Third Sunday of Lent). At the end of the reading, the
people make an appropriate response, and the celebrant explains the Word
of God. The following homily notes may be of assistance:*

Water is an element of security essential to man's life.
Not only does man need water, but it ceases to represent security for him if it is not given in conformity
with an established order. The Arabian nomad knows
that the desert is uninhabitable without certain as-
sured sources of water. The farmer knows that the
fecundity of the earth depends on the seasonal
rhythm of rains or inundations. The amount of
water is important also: it must be neither too little
nor too much. Water is not at all the fruit of man's
labor, although he has perfected to some extent his
control and rationing of this natural datum. Primitive
man spontaneously considered it just that, a datum,
a gift; and he saw the creation of the world in terms
of a divine regulating of the chaos of primeval waters.
In the faith of ancient Israel, God was seen as the

absolute master of the waters, their creator and giver. Throughout the Old Testament, water is always presented as a gift of God and not just a natural product. As God's gift, water came to be the sign of those other gifts of His: grace and Spirit, forgiveness and love, wisdom and law. It also became a sign of future salvation, when purifying and vivifying water would be poured out in abundance.

In Christ, that future salvation becomes reality. The dialogue with the Samaritan woman reveals its content: water, bread, worship in spirit, the universal harvest. Man needs water in order to live, but the gift of God which fills man reaches him at another, altogether more profound level of his being. To this gift he responds by faith: his thirst becomes a thirst for the Kingdom. In the Sacrament of Baptism, especially, the gift of God reaches its full significance. Water purifies; Baptism washes away sin. Water is a source of fecundity; Baptism is the source of new life in Christ. Water is a destructive element, a symbol of death; Baptism is a share in Christ's death and resurrection.

The celebrant then goes to the font (or basin) to bless the water, using the following prayer:

Lord our God,
Be with us as we recall the wonder of our creation
and the greater wonder of our redemption.
Bless this creature water:
it makes the seed to grow,
it refreshes us and makes us clean.
You have made of it a servant of Your loving kindness:
through water You set Your people free,
and quenched their thirst in the desert.
With water the prophets announced a new covenant
that You would make with man.
By water, sanctified in Christ,
You made our sinful nature new
in the bath that gives rebirth to everlasting life.
Let this water remind us of our Baptism
as we strive to live the mysteries of this Lent.

Save us once again
and bring us to Your promised life
through this water which is Your gift
and which now inspires our rededication.
This we ask through Christ our Lord.

After the blessing, the lector gives directions to the people: each member of the congregation comes forward individually and kneels before the priest; the priest imposes hands and says, "May the Lord renew you and keep you faithful to the Spirit we have all received." Each person then goes to the font, takes some of the water, and very deliberately makes the sign of the cross, saying, "I have been baptized in the name of the Father, and of the Son, and of the Holy Spirit. Amen." When all have completed the ceremony and returned to the pews, the priest invites them to return the following week, and the service concludes with an appropriate hymn or psalm.

SECOND SESSION: FIFTH WEEK OF LENT

At the beginning of this service, although the church itself is lighted, the sanctuary remains in darkness. Across the sanctuary entrance, or on the level near the pews, are ranged the six candles on stands that normally surround the casket at a funeral Mass. The priest wears a stole or cope of black or purple. The entrance procession takes place in silence, and the entire service is conducted in the aisle in front of the funeral candles. A lectern is set there, as well as chairs for the priest and other ministers. From his place, the priest addresses the people:

My brothers and sisters, in the saving waters of Baptism, we became children of God. But what we are to be in the future has not yet been revealed. All we know is, that when it is revealed we shall be like Him if we have kept alive in ourselves what we were taught in the beginning. Surely everyone who entertains this hope must purify himself, must try to be as pure as Christ.

If we refuse to love, then we remain dead. God's life is not in us. What we face, then, is what we confront in this service tonight: the death-that-is-in-us. Let us pray for courage to live.

(Pause for silent prayer)

God our Father, You have given us eternal life, and this life is in Your Son Jesus Christ. If we believe in Him and keep His commandments, then we have

overcome death. Help us in this Lenten season to rise
from the death in which our sins have buried us. This
we ask through Your Son Jesus Christ, who is our life
for ever and ever.

*All are seated and the lector introduces the reading, John 11: 1-45.
The text may be found in the New Lectionary for Mass, in a longer or shorter version,
under number 34-A (Fifth Sunday of Lent). After the reading, the people
stand to make an appropriate response in song: then the celebrant gives a
homily explaining the Scripture and tonight's service in the context of Lenten
conversion. The following notes may prove helpful:*

The message of the passage from John is contained in
verses 25-26: a Christian believer cannot die. In contrast to the Old Testament theme of life, John shows
that true life is possible only through resurrection.
Christ is a decisive turning point in the meaning of
life. He is the Master of Life; He is the Resurrection
and the Life. Sinless and fully faithful to the will of
the Father, Jesus Christ possessed the fullness of
eternal life. By obedience, He confronted the hour
of death, only to pass from death into the perfect life
of the Resurrection. In order to live eternally, He had
to be able to renounce this present life, to offer it
up out of love. In Jesus Christ, the material gift of
life (and its accompanying blessings and happiness)
became truly "interiorized": the true center of gravity
of life was to be found in the midst of the family of
the Father, where death can gain no entrance. Everywhere Jesus went, death retreated before Him. And
He shares this power with all those who accept Him
through faith, who are willing to follow Him: "Whoever lives and believes in me shall never die."

*After the homily, each member of the congregation comes forward to the
priest and receives from him a purple card on which the word, "DEATH,"
is written in black letters (a sufficient number of these cards may be prepared beforehand from construction paper lettered with a felt-tip pen). The
priest instructs the people that the card should serve as a reminder during
the coming week of the hopeless situation from which Christ has raised
them. They should be told to bring the cards with them when they return
next week to attend the communal Penance service on the feast of light.
As he presents the card to each person, the priest says, "May this symbol
remind you of the death from which Christ has rescued you." When all have
returned to the pews, the service concludes with the following intercessions:*

We who are present here this evening know of darkness and death: they are all too familiar elements of our human life in this world. Tonight, however, we see that death is destroyed by Jesus Christ. Let us pray that God will do away with all the death-that-is-in-us. We make our response by saying: "Give us life, God our Father!"

—we die because of sin; may the Church be a source of holiness for all men, let us pray to the Lord.

—we die because of hatred; may God lead the nations and peoples of the earth to peace that lasts, let us pray to the Lord.

—we die because of neglect; may no one here ever despair of God's love, shown for us in Jesus Christ, let us pray to the Lord.

—we die because of weakness; may this celebration strengthen us to live and work with honesty and sincerity, let us pray to the Lord.

—we die because of our mortality; may all the faithful departed, especially .... , now share in the resurrection of Christ, let us pray to the Lord.

—we die because of .... in our community; may ......(add local intention), let us pray to the Lord.

—we die because we refuse to live; may God open us tonight to receive the only Life that lasts, let us pray to the Lord.

CONCLUDING PRAYER
(from Ephesians 2: 4-10)

God our Father, You are rich in mercy and Your love for us is so great that You have brought us to life with Your Son Jesus Christ, even though we were dead in our sins. You have raised us up and given us glory so that, through all the ages, we might be living signs of Your great kindness and grace. Keep us alive, Father, through Your Son Jesus Christ, who lives and reigns with You and the Holy Spirit, forever and ever. Amen.

THIRD SESSION: WEDNESDAY OF HOLY WEEK

*All the lights in the Church are extinguished, except those which will be
necessary to allow the lector to read. The priests and ministers enter in
procession up the main aisle of the Church, preceded by the Easter Candle.
During the procession, the lector reads from the text of the Reproaches in
the Good Friday liturgy. As the procession enters the sanctuary, the lector
stops reading as soon as conveniently possible, the Easter Candle is placed
on its stand in a position of prominence, and the priests gather around the
altar facing the people. The presiding minister then addresses the people:*

Brothers and sisters, God is light and no shadow of
darkness can exist in Him. Consequently, if we were
to say that we enjoyed fellowship with Him and still
went on living in darkness, we should be both telling
and living a lie. But if we freely admit that we have
sinned, we will find God utterly reliable and straight-
forward: He forgives our sins and makes us thorough-
ly clean from all that is evil. If we take up the attitude
that "we have not sinned," we flatly deny God's
diagnosis of our condition and cut ourselves off from
what He has to say to us. Let us pray then for open
eyes and open hearts.

(Pause for silent prayer)

God our Father, You have sent the light of your life
to all men, to give them the grace of faith so that they
may have life and have it abundantly. We pray that
You will open our eyes to Christ in whom You have
made manifest Your love of men. He is a Word of
Light and the Way of Life for every person who lives
in this world. He is the Son who lives with You in
the unity of the Holy Spirit for ever and ever.

*The priests and ministers retire to their seats for the Liturgy of the Word.
The congregation is seated. The lector then introduces the reading from
John 9: 1-41 (the man born blind). The text may be found in the New
Lectionary for Mass, in a longer or shorter version, under number 31-A
(Fourth Sunday of Lent). At the end of the reading, the lights are turned
on in church and the people stand to make an appropriate sung response to
the Scripture reading. One of the priests then explains the Word of God
in the context of this celebration; the homily notes that follow provide
some points of reference:*

Light is the medium of our ordinary natural observation. It becomes, understandably, a symbol of life and living just as darkness, by contrast, signifies death and sleep. In earlier centuries, darkness was inexorable: our means of illuminating the night did not exist. In the Old Testament, the prophets described punishment in terms of the breaking of the rhythm of day and night, and of the upsurge of darkness. Darkness and sin came to be identified, while light characterized fidelity to God and Covenant. In John, light becomes Christ, who brings judgment to darkness and ends it. Since Christ's victory over darkness (sin, death), light means being one with Him. Faith is an expression of this union with the light. The opening prayer and the Gospel reading well describe the situation: we are blind dwellers in the darkness caused by our sin, and we look for Christ to shine upon us.

After the proclamation and explanation of God's Word, the following series of reflections, patterned after the General Intercession, is used to prompt those present to a consideration of their personal sinfulness and need for forgiveness:

All of us here in this church are conscious of our blindness, of our lack of power to love, of our mediocrity as Christians. Therefore, we turn to God and freely admit that we have sinned. We make our response by saying, "Father, we have sinned against you."

—We are aware of having sinned through certain definite deeds and attitudes; we have blinded ourselves to God, and therefore we pray to Him.

—We have blinded ourselves to others; things happen in our families, there are days of crisis; we feel our guilt and our insufficiency, and we turn to God and pray to Him.

—Our good intentions are often blind; we misunderstand one another deliberately, we are suspicious, we attach importance to trifling matters; we have sinned, and we turn to God and pray to Him.

—We have shared responsibility for the hatred, unfaithfulness, dishonesty and lack of respect so prev-
alent today; we blindly refuse to change and be
converted; so we turn to God and pray to Him.

—We do worse; for every failure or catastrophe in
our lives, we blame others; we point to them and
close our eyes; we are blind, and so we turn to
God and pray to Him.

*The people respond, "Father, we have sinned against you," after each
section. It would be appropriate to pause ten seconds or so between each
to give some time for personal reflection. At the end of this examination
of conscience, directions may be given to facilitate the hearing of private
confession. During the hearing of confessions, the people may be invited
to join in the singing of appropriate hymns, to emphasize the liturgical
aspects of the Sacrament and to provide an atmosphere of mutual care and
concern. After all confessions have been heard, the priests return to the
altar.*

*Those penitents who attended the previous session and received a symbolic
card may wish to emphasize their personal conversion to Christ the Light
in the following manner. When they leave the pew, before approaching one
of the priests for the Sacrament, they go to the Easter Candle, set fire to one
corner of the card and drop it to burn in the brazier set nearby for the
purpose. The Easter Candle will, of course, be situated in an accessible
place and the lector will inform the people of the meaning of this dramatic
gesture.*
*When all have returned to their pews, the main celebrant speaks the follow-
ing prayer of thanksgiving:*

Priest: The Lord be with you.

All: And also with you.

Priest: Lift up your hearts.

All: We have lifted them up to the Lord.

Priest: Let us give thanks to the Lord our God.

All: It is right to give Him thanks and praise.

Priest: Father, all-powerful and ever-living God, we do well
always and everywhere to give you thanks through Jesus
Christ our Lord. Because You love the world so much,
You sent Him to be our Savior, to deliver us from evil and
make us over into Your sons and daughters—children of
light, not of darkness. In Him, we see Your attitude toward sinners. "Love your enemies," he told us, "be

merciful, do not condemn." We easily respond to hate by hating; through thick and thin we demand our rights; we work out our anger on another person, or we become obstinately silent toward one another. Your Son Jesus Christ did not show us such an example; He behaved in a different way. His actions are our liberation and His words are Your generosity. He ate with sinners and proclaimed to them forgiveness. He was a redeemer as well as a judge. And He urged us to follow His example. On the night of that glorious day when He rose from the dead, He gave His apostles more than example. He breathed into them the Spirit of forgiveness and commissioned them to reconcile all men to God and to each other with the very power of Your own mercy.

Father, that power has been active in our midst this evening. We thank you for having sent Your Spirit and created us anew. We had sinned against You and each other, we were strangers and wanderers. Now we can pray to You with confidence, in the very words that Jesus Himself has taught us:

All: Our Father, etc.

Priest: Deliver us, Father, from every evil and grant us peace in our day. Keep us free from sin and protect us from all anxiety as we wait in joyful hope for the coming of our Savior, Jesus Christ.

All: For the Kingdom, the Power, etc.

Priest: Lord Jesus Christ, you said to your apostles: I leave you peace, my peace I give you. Look not on our sins, but on the faith of your church, and grant us the peace and unity of your kingdom where you live for ever and ever.

All: Amen.

Priest: The peace of the Lord is with you.

All: And also with you.

Priest: As a sign that we have forgiven each other, let us offer each other a sign of peace.

The service concludes with a rousing hymn of thanksgiving as the priests and ministers exit from the altar.

GENERAL HOLY WEEK SERVICE

The opening hymn is followed by a greeting and a prayer. Then, the Scripture is read and explained: John 20: 19-23, and Luke 15: 11-32. After the homily, the community gives voice to its need of reconciliation:

Priest: Lord Jesus Christ, we come to confess our failings.

People: We come with anxiety and sorrow, with hope and expectation.

Priest: Lord Jesus Christ, we come to the lonely cross.

People: And we see you stripped, we see you murdered, we see you deserted.

Priest: Lord Jesus Christ, we come to the empty tomb.

People: And we see our own death, we see our own tomb, we see our own emptiness.

Priest: Lord Jesus Christ, when we come to the empty tomb

People: We remember how we treated our parents, our friends, our neighbors, our God, and we feel sorry.

Priest: Lord Jesus Christ, when we come to the empty tomb

People: We see a hungry world before us, the pain of starving children, the guilt of war on our hands, the terror of friends without rights, and we know that we share in these evils.

Priest: Lord Jesus Christ, when we come to the empty tomb

People: We search inside ourselves and we cannot escape what we are, men caught in our selfish love, and cold hypocrisy, our depressions, our loneliness, and our frustrations.

Priest: Lord Jesus Christ, when we come to the empty tomb

People: We face you as never before, as the one forgotten, as the one oppressed, as the one pushed aside, as the one left out.

Priest: Lord Jesus Christ, when we come to the empty tomb

People: To confess our guilt, our pain, our emptiness, and to look for hope from you.

After the commissioning of the confessors, private confessions are heard, during which appropriate hymns may be sung. At the end of the confes-

sions, the following expression of reconciliation takes place:

Priest: Men of God, why do you seek the living among the dead?

People: Because we are afraid, we are uncertain, we are uncomfortable here, and we have doubts.

Priest: Do not be afraid, for he has risen from the dead, he has broken through the tomb, he has come back to life and he is here among us now. Men of God, why do you seek the living among the dead?

People: Because we feel guilty, we feel lonely, and we feel lost, for we deserted him.

Priest: Do not carry your guilt any longer, for he has taken the guilt himself, he has buried it in his grave, he has lifted it to his cross, and he is here among us now. Men of God, why do you seek the living among the dead?

People: Because our wounds are deep. We have torn away from him, we have broken with him and with our fellowmen.

Priest: Do not dwell on your wounds, for he has risen to heal you, he has risen to forgive you, he has risen to change you and bind us all together now. Men of God, he is not dead, he is risen.

People: Yes, he is risen!

Priest: He is risen!

People: And he is here!

Priest: Alleluia!

People: Alleluia!

Priest: He is risen!

People: And he is here!

After the concluding prayer and hymn, the service may continue with informal fellowship over light refreshments in a hall or cafeteria.

GOOD FRIDAY

Celebrant: In the name of the Father, and of the Son, and of the Holy Spirit.

People: Amen.

Celebrant: "Jesus came with them to a small estate called Gethsemane, and he said to his disciples, 'Stay here while I go over there to pray.' He took Peter and the sons of Zebedee with him. And sadness came over him, and great distress. Then he said to them, 'My soul is sorrowful to the point of death. Wait here and keep awake with me.' And going on a little further he fell on his face and prayed. 'My Father,' he said, 'if it is possible, let this cup pass me by. Nevertheless, let it be as you, not I, would have it.' He came back to the disciples and found them sleeping, and he said to Peter, 'So you had not the strength to keep awake with me one hour? You should be awake, and praying not to be put to the test.' " (Matthew 26: 36-42)

People: The spirit is willing, but the flesh is weak. Awaken us from our slumber.

As the celebrant goes to his place, all remain kneeling.

Leader: It is Good Friday—the most solemn and serious moment of the Christian liturgical year. We join Christians the world over to gaze into the eyes of the Son of God, our crucified Lord, realizing that we have had a part to play in His agony by our sins. With sorrow in our hearts for what we have done, we pause in the hope of hearing from His lips those merciful words uttered that day upon the cross, "Father, forgive them, for they know not what they do!" We begin this hour with a reflective preparation for individual private confession. We will end this hour with common prayers of thanksgiving and praise.

Celebrant: Let us pray:

People: From the depths I call to you, O Lord
Lord, listen to my cry for help!
Listen compassionately to my pleading!
If you never overlooked our sins, O Lord,

Lord, could anyone survive?
But you do forgive us:
for that we revere you.   (Psalm 130)

And all then are seated for the readings.

Leader: God our Father speaks to us through His Word, the Living Word, who brings light to our minds, openness to our spirits, and a change to our hearts. Let us listen to Him as He speaks to us the commandments of life which we have transgressed.

People: Speak, Lord, we long to listen to Your voice.

Reader: Scripture readings from: Matthew 5: 17-20
         John 13: 34-35
         Luke 10: 25-28

Leader: With these commandments of justice and love, Christ does not intend to weigh us down, to remove our freedom or infringe upon it. Rather, He lays open to us the way of peace and happiness which we so ardently seek and so desperately need and which He alone can give. Why is it so hard for us to understand this?

People: Your yoke, O Lord, is easy
and your burden is light,
and still we have sinned
against you and our fellowman.
Forgive us, O Lord.

Leader: It would be a tragic thing for us if our God did not forgive. He did not have to. Yet, in His love and mercy, He chooses to extend forgiveness to all who ask for it with a contrite heart. With gratitude in our hearts, let us listen to the consoling parable of the merciful father and his prodigal son.

Reader: Scripture reading from: Luke 15: 11-32.

People: There will be more rejoicing in heaven
over one repentant sinner
than over ninety-nine virtuous men
who have no need for repentance.

Celebrant: As we ask for forgiveness from our merciful Father, let us not forget these words of Christ: "Yes, if you for-

give others their failings, your heavenly Father will forgive
you yours; but if you do not forgive others, your Father
will not forgive your failings either" (Matthew 6: 14).
Knowing this, we dare to pray:

People: Our Father, etc.

*All then kneel for the Litany of Examination of Conscience; after each
petition, all respond "Lord, forgive us."*

Celebrant: For our sins of commission . . .
   For presuming so often on your mercy while ignoring
      your justice . . .
   For pretending that we are self-made, self-ruled, and self-
      saved men . . .
   For picking and choosing the convenient parts of your
      message . . .
   For closing our hearts to the promptings of your Spirit . . .
   For praying mechanically and without conviction . . .
   For sowing discord instead of love and peace . . .
   For the times we were unjust toward our neighbors . . .
   For having spoken untruthfully about others . . .
   For having revealed secret things about others . . .
   For prejudging the motives of our fellowmen . . .
   For the times we have abused our neighbor by lying
      to him . . .
   For our disrespect for person and property . . .
   For wasting your gifts of food and natural resources . . .
   For the times we gave bad example to others by our
      actions or words . . .
   For the times we have made of human love a degrading
      lust . . .
   For ridiculing those who act according to their con-
      victions . . .
   For the times we have been the cause of ill-feelings be-
      tween others . . .
   For the times we have spoken of others without con-
      sideration . . .
   For every form of selfishness . . .
   For our sins of omission . . .
   For lack of trust and confidence in you . . .
   For neglecting the use of the sacraments . . .
   For lack of devotion and participation at Mass . . .

For the times we have been ashamed to show our religious
convictions . . .

For being ignorant and uninformed in our religion through
our own fault . . .

For failing to accept our personal responsibilities in your
Church . . .

For the gifts and talents which we have failed to culti-
vate . . .

For having neglected our human dignity and that of
others . . .

For failing to see you in others . . .

For the times we have refused our help to those who
needed us . . .

For being negligent and sluggish in fulfilling the duties
of our state of life . . .

For our apathy . . .

For every injustice and failure to act in love . . .

*After a pause for personal reflection, there follows the commissioning of the
confessors.*

Celebrant: Come, my brother priests, and in the name of
Christ, let us listen to the sorrow of our people, their
failings, and their resolve to take a new direction in their
lives in Christ. Let us listen with mercy, compassion and
love, and in His name forgive and grant peace.

Leader: As the priests go to the confessionals, let us pray
together:

People: I confess to almighty God,
and to you, my brothers and sisters,
that I have sinned through my own fault
in my thoughts and in my words,
in what I have done,
and in what I have failed to do;
and I ask blessed Mary, ever virgin,
all the angels and saints,
and you, my brothers and sisters,
to pray for me to the Lord our God. Amen.

*During the time of private confessions, there is meditative silence. The
following section of prayers concludes the hour.*

Leader: God has touched us with His love. He has listened to our sorrow and extended to us His merciful forgiveness. "Let your bodies and your voices explode with joy. God is not some human concoction. He is for real! And He is here! Despite all attempts to rationalize Him out of existence He is in our world, and He reigns over our universe. The rulers of nations often ignore Him. Men of learning often pass Him by. The masses of His creatures substitute their own little gods in His place and worship the things they can see and feel. There are others who build fortresses about themselves and manifest no need for God. Our great God will not be ignored. He will not remove Himself from our world. Let us recognize His presence and fill the air with His praises" (Leslie Brandt on Psalm 47).

People: Bless the Lord, my soul,
bless His holy Name, all that is in me!
Bless the Lord, my soul,
and remember all His kindnesses:

Leader: In forgiving all your offenses, in curing all your diseases, in redeeming your life from the pit, in crowning you with love and tenderness, in filling your years with prosperity, in renewing your youth like the eagle's.

People: The Lord is tender and compassionate,
slow to anger, most loving;
His indignation does not last forever,
His resentment exists a short time only;
He never treats us, never punishes us,
as our guilt and sins deserve.

Leader: No less than the height of heaven over earth is the greatness of His love for those who fear Him; He takes our sins farther away than the east is from the west.

People: As tenderly as a father treats his children,
so the Lord treats those who fear Him;
He knows what we are made of,
He remembers that we are dust.

Leader: Man lasts no longer than grass; no longer than a wild flower he lives; one gust, and he is gone; never to be seen there again.

People: Yet the Lord's love for those who fear Him

lasts from all eternity and for ever,
as long as they keep His covenant
and remember to obey His precepts.
Bless the Lord, my soul! (Psalm 103)

Leader: "The art of forgiveness begins when you forgive
someone. It is having a humble spirit and being done
with pride and self-pity. Forgiveness works the miracle
of change. When you forgive, you change others and
you change yourself. Forgiveness should become a habit.
Forgiveness should start new. Putting off forgiveness only
deepens the wound. Life is short, time is fleeting. Today is the day to forgive" (Wilferd A. Peterson).

People: Forgive us our trespasses as we forgive those who
trespass against us, O Lord.

Leader: "The art of thanksgiving is thanksliving. It is gratitude in action. It is thanking God for the gift of life by
living it triumphantly. It is thanking God for opportuni-
ties by accepting them as a challenge to achievement. It
is thanking God for inspiration by trying to be an inspiration to others. It is adding, to your prayers of thanksgiving, acts of thanksliving" (Wilferd A. Peterson).

People: We thank You, Lord, for Your forgiveness:
help us to extend it.
We thank You, Lord, for the gift of life:
help us to live it.
We thank You, Lord, for the gift of love:
help us to spread it.

The service concludes with this Prayer of Resolution.

People: Lord, make me an instrument of Your peace.
Where there is hatred, let me sow love;
where there is injury, pardon;
where there is doubt, faith;
where there is despair, hope;
where there is darkness, light;
where there is sadness, joy.
O Divine Master,
Grant that I may not so much seek
to be consoled as to console;

to be understood as to understand;
to be loved as to love;
For it is in giving that we receive;
it is in pardoning that we are pardoned;
And it is in dying that we are born to eternal life.
(St. Francis of Assisi)

Chapter 7

A Penitential-Eucharistic Service

This chapter and the following one are the work of Rev. Vincent Inghilterra, who wishes to acknowledge: Bob Friday, Gary O'Hare, Jack Banko and Tim Goldrick, for invaluable aid and encouragement; Frank Seta and Mark Flynn, for editorial work.

INTRODUCTION

This service should be used with a small community (20-25 persons). It is especially suited for liturgical seasons and days which emphasize the need for metanoia, forgiveness, and reconciliation. To underline the fact that sin separates one from the ecclesial community, it is suggested that the penitential part of this service be held outside of the church proper, e.g. in an adjacent hall or perhaps even the vestibule. This separation has historical precedent in the canonical public penance rite of the early Church. The penitential part of the service is followed immediately by the celebration of the Eucharist. This arrangement highlights the role of the Eucharist in the forgiveness of sins and also serves to effect the actual reconciliation of the penitents with the worshipping community of the Church. The penitential service itself is divided into three parts, following the traditional divisions described by Jungmann in his historical study of the liturgical development of Penance (The Early Liturgy, p. 242).

1. CONFESSION OF GUILT

Entrance: the penitents go in procession to the location where the penitential rite proper will take place. The area should be in semi-darkness. The procession is in silence; candles might be used.

Opening Prayer: the priest composes a short communal prayer expressing the need for a change of heart, the sinfulness of mankind, the congregation's complete and total trust in the undeserved mercy of God. An appropriate example would be the collect for the Twentieth Sunday after Pentecost in the pre-1972 Roman Missal: "O Lord, grant your faithful pardon and peace, that they may be cleansed from their sins and serve you without fear through Christ our Lord."

Reading from the Word of God: the penitents are confronted with a reading from Scripture, proclaiming the mercy of God directed toward the undeserving sinner. Appropriate: Luke 7: 36-50 (penitent woman), 15: 11-32 (prodigal son), 23: 33-43 (good thief).

Response to the Word of God: this response may be included on a prayer sheet distributed before the ceremony. Parts should be assigned to both people and priest. Suggested: psalm 22 (God's everlasting love), psalm 50 (a plea for mercy), psalm 66 (trust in God).

Homily: the priest opens the Word of God to the community and shows how it applies to them.

Silent Meditation and Reflection: an opportunity for the members of the community to examine their consciences in order to determine how they have lived their Christian calling. The examination of conscience has always had a place in the penitential rite; it has been especially stressed since the twelfth century.

Communal Witness and Confession of Sinfulness: the ancient form of canonical penance included a public admission of guilt, since all sins have community implications. For this reason, the service here supplies an occasion for such an admission on the part of the community or the individual, by anyone who feels so compelled. It should be made perfectly clear, however, that one need not publicly confess particular sins, but rather give voice to general failings that have deprived the Christian message of perfect witness. To each infidelity or failure expressed, a communal refrain might be used in answer: "Lord, have mercy," "Son of David, have mercy on us," "Father, forgive us," etc.

Individual Auricular Confession: in the practice of the penitential rite of the seventh century, an opportunity was provided for those who desired to confess their sins privately. In this service, it is suggested that the individual confessions take place with the penitent directly facing and standing before the priest. Individual penances may be assigned at this point if the priest thinks it appropriate. Those who do not wish to confess privately may remain in silent meditation with the rest of the community. This period is a time of supplication and prayer. Where feasible, a shortened form of the Litany of the Saints might be sung or prayed.

2. ADMONITION, PENANCE, RECONCILIATION

Admonition: the priest addresses the reassembled community on the necessity of striving to avoid sin and give witness to the Christian calling.

Assignment of Public Penance: a representative from the community asks the priest to impose a penance on the community. Since earliest times, the penitential rite has included some sort of assigned penance in order to make restitution for what has been destroyed by sin. Suggestion: a communal recitation of psalm 33 and an act of charity to be performed either by each individual or by teams (family, organizations, etc.) at a time suitable and convenient. Those who have already been assigned a penance privately are invited to join the community in the public penance.

Recitation of Psalm 33: the alternate recitation of the psalm by the community is a form of public penance and is in accord with the spirit of the early penitential rites.

The Reconciliation: obviously, if freedom to confess privately has been observed and yet the communal sacramental absolution is to be employed, some arrangement will have to be made to prevent ambiguity and confusion. It is suggested that those who have confessed be invited to come forward and kneel before the priest who will impose hands and give them absolution. A general blessing may be then given to all the community.

3. CELEBRATION OF THE EUCHARIST

Once the penitential rite is completed, the priest invites all those who were formerly separated from the worshipping community to join in the celebration of the Eucharist as a sign of reconciliation.

Entrance: in song, all move in procession into the church proper. When everyone is in place, the celebrant begins immediately with the opening prayer, a liturgy of the Word on mercy and reconciliation, a brief homily that will lead those present to engage in the Eucharist with joyful love and thanksgiving for God's mercy and goodness. The Mass then continues as usual.

An alternate to the above arrangement would be to use the liturgy of the Word as a penitential preparation, provide opportunity for individual confessions after the homily, and insert "Admonition-Penance-Reconciliation" segment immediately before the Preparation of the Gifts.

Chapter 8

Special Theme
Penance Services

RETURN TO THE LORD

The participants gather in the church. The lector or principal minister introduces the theme. Then the entrance hymn is sung.

Priest: O God, most merciful Father,
    We come together to confess our blindness.
    You remember that we are dust
    and You know our waywardness.
    Have mercy on us, O God.
    Cleanse us of our selfishness.
    Purify our dedication in Your service.
    Remove the barriers that divide us,
    the shortcomings that spring from human weakness.
    Teach us to forgive and bear with others
    as You forgive and bear with us.
    Let our hearts of stone become hearts of flesh,
    so that there may be no obstacle
    to our love for You and for one another.

Lector: Isaiah 40: 1-11 (or, possibly, Evely's *That Man Is You,*
    pp. 135-140)

People: He shall feed His flock like a shepherd,
and He shall gather the lambs with His arms
and carry them in His bosom,
and gently lead those that are with young.
Come unto Him all you that labor,
come unto Him you that are heavy laden
and He will give you rest.
Take His yoke upon you and learn of Him,
for He is meek and humble of heart,
and you shall find rest for your souls.

Lector: Luke 15: 1-3, 11-32

People: O Lord Jesus Christ, we give You thanks
that You have come to call us sinners.
You forgive our guilt and desire to be
our companion at the table of the Eucharist.
For it is in the breaking of the bread
that we recognize You are in our presence.
It is in the drinking of the cup of Your blood
poured out for the forgiveness of sins
that we find reconciliation with You
and with our brothers and sisters.

After a brief homily, there may be a silent pause for an examination of conscience, followed by a litany of pardon:

Priest: If we say we have no sin, we deceive ourselves and the truth is not in us.

People: Hear, O Lord, and grant us pardon. (Repeat after each phrase)

Priest: With Peter the Apostle we say: Depart from me, Lord, for I am a sinful man. (Response)

Mindful of Mary Magdalen, Peter and the thief on the cross, we come to You in confidence. (Response)

You, O Christ, are our advocate, to plead our case before the Father. (Response)

You, O Lord, have taken our sins upon Yourself; in Your body, You bore them on the wood of the cross. (Response)

During the period of individual confessions, the congregation may sing or

remain silent in prayer.
After the confessions, a public penance is assigned, and the service con-
cludes with a hymn of thanksgiving.

GOD'S PEACE

Leader: We who have gathered here claim to believe in
Jesus Christ; we know the power He has given to His
Church to bring men back to His peace from their sinful
ways.

After the entrance hymn, the celebrant offers the following prayer:

Priest: God our Father, at Your invitation, we have come
together as one family. We come not in fear but in trust
and confidence, because of Your great goodness. We
confess that we have done wrong by not caring when
we should have cared, by our indifference to the needs
of people, by hating or ignoring, by misusing Your gifts
and love and friendship.

Through the mercy and goodness of Christ our Lord,
forgive us for not doing the good You command, and for
doing the evil that You forbid. Restore peace and joy to
our hearts; set our minds on justice and love. One in the
Spirit, may we grow to full sonship and bring peace to
the world in which we live.

Lector: Isaiah 42: 1-7 or 43: 1-14

Leader: We wish to serve You, our living God, in the name
of Your Son.

People: Give us strength, Lord, give us peace. (After each
phrase)

Leader: Forgive our sins, Lord, forgive our failings; they are
many, Lord. (Response)

You have given us so much, Lord, and still we fail to
love. (Response)

Our faith is weak, Lord, teach us to trust in You. (Response)

Sometimes we are petty, Lord, narrow in mind and heart;
give us Your vision, Lord. (Response)

Lector: Hebrews 4: 14-16

After an appropriate response, the priest delivers a brief homily which is then followed by a litany of pardon:

Leader: Since we do not search Your will,

People: Forgive us, O Lord. (After each petition)

Leader: Since we are willful,
    Since we do not wish,
    When we hate or fail to love,
    When we choose hate over love,
    When we are so sure we cannot doubt,
    When we are so doubtful we cannot act,
    For being too involved,
    For remaining uncommitted,
    For forgiving our own wrongs,
    For not forgiving those of others,
    For those we have excluded,
    For not caring about our world,
    For what is in our hearts,
    For what is not in our hearts,
    For our sins against each other,
    For our sins against all others.

During the period of individual confessions, the congregation may sing or remain silent in prayer. After the public penance, the service concludes with a hymn of thanksgiving.

THE SPIRIT OF FORGIVENESS

Leader: Our Lord Jesus Christ calls us to conversion in His Spirit. He cries: "Come to Me, all you who thirst and hunger. Come to Me, all you who need justice and mercy. Come to Me, so that you can proclaim to others the wonders that the Father has done for you."

After the entrance hymn, the opening prayer:

Priest: Lord Jesus Christ, send Your Spirit which You promised to Your Church, so that we may come back to You, to Your simple peace and Your gracious light. Strengthen us to live the lives You have given us.

Lector: Isaiah 65: 1-7, or James 4: 1-7

An appropriate response would be a period of silent reflection on personal sinfulness and need for repentance.

Lector: Hosea 4: 1-8

After an appropriate response, the priest gives a brief homily. Before the hearing of individual confessions, each member of the congregation advances and kneels at the feet of the priest who says to each:

Priest: May the Spirit of God strengthen you to be converted and return to the Lord.

After the confessions, as a sign of renewal, all make the following declarations:

People: My God, I believe that You are the one God. I believe that Your Son Jesus Christ became man and died for our sins. I believe that He will come again to judge the living and the dead.

My God, I rely on Your power and mercy to obtain forgiveness of my sins. I rely on Your gracious help in this life, so that You will call me to Your Kingdom in the next life.

My God, I love You with my entire being. I wish to direct all my energies to living for You and serving You in Your Church and in this world.

After the public penance, the service concludes with a hymn of thanksgiving.

DEDICATION TO SERVICE

Leader: We have tried to serve You, Lord, but You know our failings. We come before You to seek the soothing peace, the gracious mercy, the renewed strength which You can give.

After the opening hymn, the priest recites an opening prayer.

Lector: Ephesians 5: 1-20, or James 4: 1-14

The reading is followed by a corporate examination of conscience:

Leader: For failure to respond to the needs of the people for whom we have dedicated our lives.

People: Have mercy, Lord, for we are sinners. (After each phrase)

Leader: For failure to witness to the poverty of Christ, for our emphasis on pleasure, comfort and convenience. (Response)

For placing personal preference above community needs. (Response)

For being satisfied with mediocrity. (Response)

For lack of creativity and apostolic interest. (Response)

For apathy toward the social and political problems of our times. (Response)

For forgetting those whom we do not see, who rely on our prayers. (Response)

For living the lie of ourselves instead of the love of God. (Response)

For contributing to the absurdity and confusion of man's situation. (Response)

For taking so much forgiveness and giving little in return. (Response)

Priest: We have confessed openly our sinfulness. Now, let us seek the peace that Christ gives to the penitent.

People: Lord, open my mouth to praise You in humble confession; fuse in my heart a new spirit.

Priest: In Your sight, we are guilty, Lord; before all men, too, we bear blame for those actions which separate us from You and from each other. Through our sins, life grows cold in Your living body, the Church. By your love and mercy, stir up within us the true spirit of penance. Make of us a community of love and service. We turn now to You and all our brothers and sisters who are the Church:

People: I confess to almighty God,
and to you, my brothers and sisters, etc.

Priest: May almighty God have mercy on us,

forgive us our sins,
and bring us to everlasting life.

People: Amen.

Individual confessions are now heard. During this period, the people may sing or remain silent in prayer for each other. After the confessions, all stand for the following reading:

Lector: John 20: 19-30

After a meditative pause, the priest prays:

Priest: Lord Jesus Christ, we thank You for standing in our midst this evening to bring us the gift of Your peace. You have forgiven all our sins and now You send us as You sent the Apostles, just as the Father sent You. We are strengthened by this trust and confidence, but we know our weakness. Therefore, we turn with You to the Father and we pray as You have taught us:

People: Our Father, etc.

The service concludes with the exchange of the sign of peace and a final hymn of thanksgiving.

RECONCILIATION

The people enter in silent procession, carrying candles. When all are in place standing, the priest says:

Priest: Assembled here as God's redeemed people, let us enter into the mystery of His unlimited love for us. (Pause) Lord, I am a sinful man, a weak human being; and I ask for Your forgiveness, as well as the forgiveness of Your people here assembled. Make me worthy to be Your servant and to represent Your Church.

All kneel and recite the following prayer:

People: Come, Holy Spirit, fill the hearts of Your people and enkindle in them the fire of Your love. Come upon us, Your people, that we may be created in Your likeness, and let the face of the earth be renewed. Let Your kingdom come!

All are seated for the reading.

Lector: I John 1: 8 - 2: 2

As an appropriate response, it is suggested that psalm 31 be recited alternately.

Priest: God, most merciful Father, we have come together to confess our sinfulness before You. Help us to be mindful of our evil, as individuals and as groups. We ask this in the name of Your Son and in His Spirit.

People: Amen.

Priest: My brothers and sisters, we will now take a few moments to reflect on our sinfulness and our infidelity.

After a period of silence, one of the congregation initiates the litany of personal and collective infidelities. All are invited to participate, if so moved. After each accusation, the community responds, "Lord, have mercy." All then stand.

Lector: Luke 24: 36-47

Individual confessions are now heard. At the end of the confessions, after the absolution, each member of the congregation approaches the priest who imposes hands and says:

Priest: May God keep you free from every sin and obstacle that would hinder your union with Him and with the community of His people on earth.

All then recite the Our Father, exchange the sign of peace, and sing a final hymn of thanksgiving.

GOD'S MERCY AND LOVE

The ministers of the service greet the penitents as they arrive in the vestibule of the church. All remain there for the beginning of the celebration, when the main celebrant says:

Priest: God our Father, You have said to Your people: "Wash yourselves clean and put away misdeeds from before My eyes. Cease evil doing and learn to do good. Make justice your aim by redressing the wronged; hear the orphan's plea and defend the widow." We, Your sinful servants, have received Your word and respond to Your call. We beg You, Father, to hear our plea and allow us to return to Your merciful presence. (Pause)

Come now, my brothers and sisters; let us set things right before one another and before our God. Though our sins be like scarlet, they may become as white as snow; though they be crimson red, they will become white as wool.

All enter the church while singing a hymn of hope in the mercy and love of the Father. Once all are in place, the liturgy of the Word begins.

Lector: Leviticus 4: 13-21

After an appropriate response, the second reading:

Lector: Luke 15: 11-32

In the homily, the preacher should show that man's sin is both individual and communitarian, that God loves sinners and chooses them to be His people, that we need only turn to the Father and He will forgive. A call for repentance concludes the homily:

Priest: As we have come together, a sinful people chosen by God, let us now reflect upon the ways in which we have turned against God and each other.

After a period of reflection, the penitents disperse throughout the church, an action historically symbolic of the traditional separation of the sinner from the community. The penitents go to confession and receive individual penances. While the act of reconciliation is taking place, the rest of the community prays for all sinners, a prayer of intercession in which the Church is constantly engaged. After the sacrament, all return to the body of the Church where the celebrant invites them to join in the praying of the Our Father. He then prays over the assembled community with outstretched hands:

Priest: The Lord has called us and we have heard Him, and He has delivered us from all our sins and failures. Look to Him that you may not blush with shame. Keep your tongues from evil and your lips from speaking guile. We were alienated, now we are reunited as friends—indeed, as sons and daughters, reinstated in the Father's house. Let us bless the Lord always and keep His covenant of love always in our hearts.

After this prayer, the ministers together give a general blessing and dismiss the people, charging them to spread the love and mercy of God which they have experienced. The recessional hymn should express both praise and worship of God.

Appendix

A Pastoral Letter on Public Penance

This pastoral letter was published by the Bishops of Holland on March 16, 1965.

Brothers and Sisters in Christ. As the gospels testify, John the Baptist preached a baptism of penance for the remission of sins. Mark wrote with reference to the first public appearance of Jesus in Galilee, "the time has come and the reign of God is near; repent, and believe this good news" (Mk 1: 15). Everyone wno reads the scriptures feels the call to conversion, to change his life, and to follow Jesus. There is no exception from this call.

Conversion is realized most basically in baptism. Through baptism we belong to Christ, we live our life as Christ lived his: with faith, in dependence on the heavenly Father, in community with our neighbors. But we are men in the process of change, men of pilgrimage. Seldom does our total commitment to the kingdom of God and the salvation of our neighbor reach to the limits of its demands. Our best intentions often clash with our weakness and our selfishness. Each and every one of us shares responsibility for the fact that the church exercises so little attraction among so many people, for because of our sins her growing expansion is blocked. The opposition in our country, the anguish and hunger in the world would decrease if our likeness with Christ would increase. He became man so as to concretely show the love of God for man, and to make such a love tangible in authentic human conduct. He exemplified a sincere and unselfish life. He has called every man to strive to become a good man. His death on the cross was the sacrifice of his life. He has assembled into his church all who believe in his name and promise to live a life similar to his.

As we become aware of our vocation as Christians, there follows the conviction that we continually need the forgiveness of God and men. We all have faults. But we can rejoice in these words of Christ to Peter, "I do not say to you seven times, but seventy times seven" (Mt 18: 22), that is, always. We should repeat with the prodigal son: "Father, I have sinned against heaven and you. I no longer deserve to be called your son" (Lk 15: 21).

Whoever is aware of his own need for forgiveness learns to forgive. It is only possible to forgive when one really knows himself.

We all recognize that we have sorrowed others, notwithstanding the best intentions. Likewise we know how desperately men seek human happiness. Therefore should we not trust the good intentions of all others? Should we not show each other the spirit of forgiveness, so as to exemplify the goodness and mercy of God?

Surely it would be an impoverishment of the Christian spirit in family and social life if we did not value mutual forgiveness as Christ himself did when he said: "So when you are presenting your gift at the altar, if you remember that your brother has any grievance against you, leave your gift right there before the altar and go and make up with your brother; then come back and present your gift" (Mt 5: 23-24). We must try, insofar as possible, to foster reconciliation with others and to make reparation for offenses. Confession cannot dispense us from this obligation; rather, it should foster this effort. When we have failed, we must confess this failure and ask for forgiveness.

The church and holy scripture have always taught that sins are forgiven in many ways; the liturgical and extraliturgical forms, far from being opposed, are complementary. Among such forms are the authentic celebration of the eucharist, the silent prayer of self-examination, fasting, almsgiving, the admission of fault and request for forgiveness from our neighbor. All these are summarized and confirmed, as it were, in the absolution of the priest in the sacrament of penance.

In recent times, besides the well-known private confession, the public celebration of penance is becoming more and more accepted. By this we understand a celebration where Christians publicly confess before God and man that they are sinners; the priest invites them to this through a meditation on life and a request for the mercy of God on all of good will. In this celebration there is no specific confession of sins, nor is there the absolution which is given in private confession.

These types of celebration can be enriched in many ways. It can be helpful to come together, to seek integrity and fraternity, to mutually hear the admission of faults. This celebration can become the clear sign that men are reconciled, a sign that energizes the renewal of our lives. All will understand how this celebration can be for many a great help in the formation of their conscience and the development of a mature sense of responsibility. Also, it offers the priest an opportunity to teach Christians "to see in their hearts, beyond their deeds and attitudes," and so to appreciate the precise value of the connection between intimate feelings and external conduct.

Jesus says in the gospel: "For wherever two or three are gathered as my followers, I am there among them" (Mt 18: 20). The Lord is present and so we believe that all who are sincere obtain forgiveness. Therefore the priest has the right to proclaim that forgiveness in a general prayer of intercession. As a matter of fact, we believe that whenever man, influenced by God's grace, is sorry for his sins, forgiveness is always obtained even before the absolution reserved to private confession is pronounced over him. But in the same way we believe that whenever there is no repentance, there is no forgiveness.

But if public celebrations of penance are on the increase, it does not follow that private confession should become

obsolete. Rather it is desired that this celebration should be
a school wherein we learn to make our confession before a
priest, the representative of both God and the community
of men, a deeper, more personal event. Particularly during
Lent, the time of preparation for Easter, we should ask whether
the sacrament of penance is a real event in our lives. Going
to confession is an encounter in which we meet God as a
Father who understands and desires a greater intimacy with
us. It is a journey back to the father's house, or in other
words, a journey to again find understanding, concern, and
interest. Christ speaks of the sheep that is lost, tired, and
alone. He goes in search and carries the lost sheep back to
light and warmth.

Confession has to take place in prayer: only in prayer
can it be a true encounter with the Lord. It is needless to say,
then, that haste on the part of either the penitent or the confessor must be avoided. Both must try to create an atmosphere
that favors a real human contact, in such a way that repentance
and forgiveness are experientially realized. Perhaps confessions have left us unsatisfied because in our hearts there remained the feeling that our confession was not authentic,
that it did not fully express our state of sin or weakness.
Perhaps we have said many things without really confessing
them.

A regular and well-prepared confession will be helpful for
everyone who wishes to grow in the Christian life, who seeks
a spiritual guide, and who wants to hear the proclamation of
mercy and forgiveness in the deepest part of his being.

Let us remember that there is always the obligation to
explicitly mention every mortal sin in confession. All should
ask whether they are evading real obligations. Likewise we
should ask whether we are actually willing to submit our
personal judgment to the control and judgment of others, of
the church. We must ask ourselves whether we are not avoid-
ing a sincere confession of our faults. A grave fault demands
a greater reparation than an inadvertent act which does not
provoke grave consequences. Do we consider ourselves
seriously guilty? Let us have the courage to admit it. Let us
recognize that we have damaged the church and have hin-
dered her growth. In this case a personal confession through
the sacrament of penance is in order. Anyone in this situation

who confesses before a priest who knows how to listen to him and who has the power to forgive in the name of God will experience how beneficial, liberating, and consoling private confession can be.

We express the desire that all of us who form the church of Holland may acquire, during these weeks before Easter, a more vivid feeling of the presence of sin in our lives, and that this feeling may mature by means of the celebrations of public penance, which will culminate finally in a sincere and personal private confession.

1. The institution of public celebrations of penance deserves our positive approval. Hence we recommend that all who have the care of souls call the faithful together from time to time, for instance during Advent and Lent, for public celebrations of penance. But the celebrant must first endeavor to have a precise idea of the sense and the value of these practices. Likewise it is necessary to provide the faithful with careful instruction and serious preparation before initiating these celebrations.

2. The public celebration of penance should not be developed at the expense of private confession. The public celebration in itself and through the words of the priest should be like an invitation towards a more personal, more authentic private confession.

3. Every priest hearing private confessions must make a special effort to act in such a way that the sacrament is received in an atmosphere of peace and prayer, so that the Christian can express himself authentically and a true pastoral contact between the priest and penitent may be brought about. In both public proclamation and personal direction, the priest, looking first to the dispositions of the human heart, will carefully and respectfully help the faithful in a way that facilitates sincere conversion.

It is also advisable that the priest with care of souls make use of the celebration of public penance to awaken in the faithful an ever-increasing awareness of the social and ecclesial dimensions of human guilt. In this way they may help to form their conscience with greater depth and make them understand more fully how every one of us, personally and collectively, is responsible for every existing sin in the human community.

4. The church has always taught that man, even before private confession, can be forgiven by the sincerity of his repentance. Likewise the church believes that only the man who truly repents can receive the forgiveness of his sins in the sacrament of penance.

5. A general prayer of intercession to invoke the mercy and forgiveness of God is most suitable for the public celebration of penance. The use of the formula of absolution, reserved by the church for private confession, cannot be justified.

6. For various reasons, for example, the presence of a great number of the faithful at public celebrations in the parishes, it does not seem advisable to provide those present with the opportunity to confess their sins in private and to receive absolution during the actual service. But if the community is small, a celebration of confession can be organized, that is, a service which includes individual private confession and absolution, so that only the preparation and thanksgiving are in common.

7. We must uphold firmly the obligation to confess in private all mortal sins. It is recommended that this obligation be taught in such a way that the faithful will accept it not as an external obligation, but rather as an expression of an internal necessity which demands the personal confession of mortal sins.

8. For the present, it is advisable not to preach on the question of the sacramentality of the public celebration of penance, since this is still a controverted theological problem. It is obvious that for every sacrament in the strict sense of the word, the determination and recognition of the church's magisterium are required.

Nevertheless, it would be desirable that the priest with the care of souls gradually introduce the faithful to a deeper and broader understanding of the notion of sacramentality, so that they may better understand the affirmation "Christ is sacrament" and not continue to ignore the fact that our whole Christian life and conduct have a sacramental meaning.